# A Thought for Each Day of the Year

BY THE

REV. FR. MARIN DE BOYLESVE, S.J.

# A Thought for Each Day of the Year

by Rev. Fr. Marin de Boylesve, S.J.

Originally translated from the French by Wilfridus
and published by Burns and Oates in 1877.

This edition edited and annotated
by E.A. Bucchianeri, 2021.

Batalha Publishers
Fátima, Portugal

ISBN: 978-989-33-1995-6

## PREFACE

Many Catholics abstain from meditating upon the truths of religion, under the plea that they have no time to spare.

Books of meditation abound, but the subjects are too much developed; and they say they have only a few moments at their disposal after morning prayer.

It is proposed to offer a reading, the length of which can frighten no one. One or two moments will suffice to read the subject, less than a quarter of an hour's reflection will bring it home.

Each day's reading will consist of a text from the Gospel of the Sunday, a thought upon the text, a prayer inspired by that thought, and a practical resolution.

Some of the reflections and resolutions are often repeated because they are repeated in the Gospels, and are so essential that they cannot be dwelt upon too often.

As the Ecclesiastical Year commences in Advent, this course of meditations is begun on the first Sunday in the Liturgical Year.

Fr. Marin de Boylesve

# Table of Contents

## ADVENT

Due to the movable nature of Easter, etc. there may be only Three Sundays After the Epiphany, or, there may as many as Six Sundays After the Epiphany before the period of Septuagesima occurs, which is the week marking the 63 – 70 Day Period before Easter Sunday.

You will have to look at a calendar and see when the Lenten Season and Easter will be in the year to calculate the number of Sundays After the Epiphany that will occur.

To make it simple, you can calculate 'backwards' from Ash Wednesday. See when Ash Wednesday will fall in the year you are making these meditations – Ash Wednesday occurs the Wednesday after Quinquagesima Sunday. The Sunday before that is Sexagesima Sunday, and the Sunday before that is Septuagesima. You then count how many Sundays After the Epiphany occur before you reach Septuagesima. This is the number of Sundays that occur after the Feast of the Epiphany (January 6).

If there are are only Three Sundays After Epiphany in a year, then when that week of meditations is completed skip ahead to Septuagesima.

If there are Four Sundays After Epiphany in the year, then do that week of meditation before continuing straight to Septuagesima, etc.

The Epiphany (Week)

## SEPTUAGESIMA – Liturgical Prelude

## PASSION TIDE

ೞಙ❀ಲಚಜ

## * <u>(Optional Mediations for The Fifth Sunday After Easter / Ascension Week)</u>

Apparently, Fr. Marin included an extra week here, and therefore we can indicate them as an optional set, which is useful for varying the cycle of meditations each year.

ಖಖ⊕ಌಡ

## PENTECOST

**NOTE:** due to the movable feast of Easter, etc., there may be more than 24 Sundays After Pentecost in a given year. The extra Sundays and their weeks are first 'filled in' with weeks from the Sundays After the Epiphany depending on the number of extra Sundays, then the Pentecost Cycle is completed with the Last / Twenty-Fourth Sunday After Pentecost.


*What to do at this point:*

First, count how many Sundays there are after Pentecost Sunday in the year you are making these meditations.

* Following the original Latin Mass Calendar, if there are only 24 Sundays after Pentecost, then after the Twenty-Third Sunday, you may turn straight to The Twenty-Fourth Sunday After Pentecost, which is the

last, and complete the Pentecost cycle.

- If there are 25 Sundays After Pentecost, turn to the Sixth Sunday After the Epiphany for that week (#92), then finish the Pentecost cycle with the Twenty-Fourth Sunday After Pentecost (#387).
- If there are 26 Sundays After Pentecost, turn to the Fifth and Sixth Sundays After the Epiphany (#85, #92), then finish with the Twenty-Fourth Sunday After Pentecost (#387).
- If there are 27 Sundays After Pentecost, fill in with the Fourth, Fifth and Sixth Sundays after the Epiphany (#78, #85, #92) then finish the Pentecost cycle with the Twenty-Fourth Sunday After Pentecost (#387).
- If there are 28 Sundays After Pentecost, turn to the Third, Fourth, Fifth, and Sixth Sundays After the Epiphany (#71, #78, #85, #92), then finish the Pentecost cycle with the Twenty-Fourth Sunday after Pentecost (#387).

# About the Author

Fr. Marin de Boylesve was born on November 28, 1813 at the Château de la Coltrie in the commune of Saint-Lambert de la Potherie near Angers. He came from a distinguished aristocratic family whose name can be traced back many centuries as seen in Abbé Jean-Baptiste Ladvocat's *Dictionnaire historique portatif* (1755). Fr. Marin descended directly from Eslienne Boyliaue (or Boilyeve), the great statesman and the principal adviser of St. Louis IX, King of France. Other illustrious ancestors included intrepid knights, one in particular also named Marin joined the cause of King Henry IV. After the Battle of Arques, the king called him 'his beloved knight', granted him a heredity knighthood in 1597, then was made Seigneur de la Maurouziere in 1598 thereby granting him the right to add three gold fleur-de-lis to the top of his arms and bear the signs of the Order of St. Michel in his escutcheon. He was also appointed lieutenant-general of Anjou and councillor of state as a reward for his dedication. Another Marin Boylesve appears in the family line, the third to hold the name, and was in service to King Louis XIV as manager of his hôtel. Loyal to the French King and to their Catholic faith, many members of the family were forced to emigrate during the French Revolution, but some members stayed behind in their beloved France. Fr. de Boylesve would recall a favourite family story, of how his grandmother was imprisoned in Angers by the Revolutionaries and managed a daring escape on the road during a prisoner transfer to the local castle.

While she pretended to pick up a dropped package, a solider kicked her into the ditch. She took the opportunity to flee to a nearby house. However, when they threatened to imprison those harbouring escaped prisoners, she bravely marched straight in to the Revolutionary Office and gave herself up to ensure the safety of those who sheltered her. The revolutionaries did not dare risk upsetting the populace as her father was the former mayor of Angers before the Revolution and loved by the people. They decided to let her return to her father's house.

Fr. de Boylesve was the last direct descendant of his distinguished line, having followed the call to enter the Company of Jesus, or Jesuits, which also is a remarkable story of a predestined vocation. The Jesuits were persecuted due to fears they were growing in power and wealth. Pressured by the royal courts of Europe, Pope Clement XIV suppressed the Society, forcing members of the order to renounce their vows and go into exile. They were expelled from France in 1764. Fr. de Boylesve's mother, Clémentine de Livonnière, made a solemn promise on the day of her wedding that if God permitted the Jesuits to return to France and she was granted a son, she would offer him to the order and entrust him to it. As mentioned, Fr. Marin was born in 1813, a year before 1814 when Pope Pius VII restored the Society. Tragedy struck when Marin's father died, Marin was only ten months old at the time, but keeping her promise his mother dutifully sent him for his education at the age of ten to the Jesuit Fathers of Montmorillon. The moment he arrived at the school and saw a Jesuit for the first time who happened to be the Superior of the college Fr. Michel Le Blanc, he heard an inner voice say to him: "Little one, that is what you will be."

Fr. de Boylesve entered the school as a student and was destined never to leave the Jesuits. In 1831 he turned eighteen, a year after the July Revolution of 1830, which saw the rightful king to the French throne Charles X overthrown. His heir, Henry V the 'Miracle Child', was forced into exile at the age of ten,  his throne usurped by the man who had been approached to be his regent, Louis-Philippe, Duke of Orléans. The events of the times burned the hearts of the faithful as the historical church of the royal family, Saint-Germain-l'Auxerrois, was profaned. Paris was sacked, and wayside devotional crosses and shrines over large areas of France were destroyed as Catholic legitimist symbols of Charles X, even those which had no royal significance or connection to the king.

Fr. Marin had just completed his schooling when he formally announced his decision to enter the Society, the historic events of the previous year and their aftermath no doubt influencing his decision. Writing to his grandmother he declared:   "The course of my studies completed I could not remain without doing anything. God will ask us for an exact account of all the moments He gives us. Full of this thought I ardently wished to serve my country and the Church especially. At a time when both are in such great peril, as a Frenchman and as a Christian, I felt the need to throw myself into the thick of the fray.  To take place in the first rows under the banners of religion whose triumph alone can bring glory and happiness back to my homeland, to serve immediately under my first head Jesus Christ, to be one of His companions, seemed to me the most glorious at the same time as most useful for my neighbour. Immense advantages, treasures of happiness and glory, the hundredfold from this life of all that I would give to the Lord, all of these promised in the gospel by Jesus Christ, strongly attracted me to be generous. What more could I do than give myself? (...)"

His family strongly opposed, especially as he was the last direct heir to the Boylesve house, but his mother let him go despite the great sacrifice, no doubt she understood God was accepting her promise to give him to the Jesuits, and not just for his education but now was asking for his whole life, a bitter dreg for her down to the last drop of the cup.

He entered the Novitiate in 1831 at Estavayer in the canton of Fribourg in Switzerland with two other students. As they arrived at their new school, they rang the doorbell at the moment the house clock struck three. The Father who received them remarked: "You are entering at the hour of the Sacred Heart." This introduction to a new school would once again give Fr. de Boylesve a sign regarding the future work he would one day accomplish, although on this occasion he did not know it at the time. He made his first vows at the Maison du Passage on October 10, 1833. He studied philosophy and then in 1835 became a supervisor at the Collège de Mélan, a position he held for one year. He remained in the same college until 1842 where he was in succession professor of grammar, humanities and rhetoric. He thoroughly enjoyed his work with the students, writing in 1837:

"I find this job a lot of fun, despite the hardships that come with it. I have forty students; I love them and I try to spare nothing to make them good Christians, educated Christians capable of one day rendering true service to religion and to the state. It is the sight of such a noble ending that sustains and animates me." In the same letter he continues, regarding his concern for his family, "(...) what the only important thing is, is everyone behaving well and does he remember the motto of the family, RELIGIO, PATRIA? For me who gave up everything, even my name which will be extinguished in my person, I remember it, and God grant that I am consumed and that I use myself in the service of one and of the other."

Although renouncing his aristocratic life he never gave up its noble spirit represented by the family motto, an ardent loyalty to the Catholic faith of his forefathers and his country. In the title pages of his texts he included the family crest of three crosses and motto: RELIGIO, PATRIE – "Faith and Country". Those who knew him and his 'military' style ways said he was just like the loyal intrepid knights of old.

At the end of 1842 he returned to France. He took theology courses at Laval for four years. Instinctively he was drawn to the writings of St. Thomas Aquinas and steered clear of new systems that deviated from the philosophical teachings of the Seraphic Doctor. In 1846 theology training completed, Fr. Boylesve was sent by his superiors to Angers, then in his third year at Notre-Dame d'Ay. In 1848 he was appointed to Brugelette, where he occupied the chair of philosophy. One student who fondly recalled Fr. de Boylesve and his time at Brugelette said his arrival was providential. His classes were easy to follow his manner clear and crisp, but this is not all that gained the respect of the students. In 1848 they were restless as revolution was in the air, Louis-Philippe I, who had overthrown Catholic King Charles X was now in his own turn overthrown. Rising above and beyond what was required of his philosophy courses, Fr. Boylesve seized the opportunity like a knight-commander of old to direct the lazy students yet bursting with energy towards something constructive: Catholic action to fashion them into vigorous young men of service for Church and country. With his apostolic action he captivated the students with his literature classes, speaking on many subjects from philosophy, history, politics both ancient and modern. He particularly drew them with his catechism lessons on the Council of Trent, his clarity and enthusiasm captivating them.

As Fr. de Boylesve loved his students he was equally admired and loved by them, earning the nickname 'The Captain' as a mark of respect. The students composed a military style tune for his birthday, the refrain remaining popular and hummed everywhere: "Courageous Captain, lead us into battle." A student recalls: "I understood all that was apostolic about his action on us. We can sum it up by saying that he made it his mission to preach to us always and everywhere the contemplation of Saint Ignatius on the Reign of Jesus Christ as it is given in the Exercises." In 1851 Fr. Boylesve was sent to Vannes where he was made prefect of studies, his nickname 'The Captain' following him. In October 1853 he left the post and resumed teaching philosophy, a position that he would keep for a long time, either in Poitiers or in Vaugirard.

Known to be quiet and reserved when on his own, it was another matter when he was teaching or publicly speaking. He was incapable of remaining silent or softening his direct manner of expression when it was a question of truth, and did not hold back when it came to defend the Faith and the Church against unbelievers, becoming as noted like his knight-ancestor of old, charging forth to give chase and defeat any bold rascal on the field of battle albeit with his tongue and writings rather than with a literal sword. His attitude is quaintly summed up by the art critique he once gave of the statue of the fountain of St. Michael in Paris, complaining with slight annoyance that the mighty archangel was made to look too carefree and benevolent when dispatching Satan: "See then, it is that he seems to spare him!" He was also a zealous worker and relished activity. He once wrote: "I challenge my superiors to give me too much work." In addition to his religious duties and teaching, he was a prolific writer, his output seeming to have no end. He wrote on a myriad of subjects and in different genres, from devotional booklets and pamphlets to history, literature, philosophy, Biblical dramas, summaries of the Church Fathers and Doctors, his own sermons, studies of the Scriptures, Our Lady, the Exercises of St. Ignatius just to name a few, there were always more plans for further works in progress, his room filled with notes and notebooks. He was always studying as well, also making it a practise to read through the entire Bible every year. One might call him a workaholic in today's terms, but it was noted he believed in a time and a place for everything and diligently managed his hours. He enjoyed recreation time, especially going for walks, and did not sacrifice rest. Despite his zest for work, he disapproved of a few young professors who sacrificed too much sleep and recreation time for their studies, endangering their health. Yet, while sparing of his time, he was ever charitable and ready to help another all for the glory of God.

In September 1870 Fr. de Boylesve was sent to the College of Le Mans, Notre-Dame de Sainte-Croix, when the Franco-Prussian war was raging and France suffered the indignity of invasion. The humiliation felt by the country also struck the pious and patriotic Fr. de Boylesve  to  the  core:  "I  searched  through  the memories of my life; I do not remember ever having felt greater pain than this, not even when I learned of my mother's death. This humiliation of France, the eldest daughter of the Church, thus succumbing before Prussia, the eldest daughter of Protestantism, in the face of the whole world, is something unheard of."

*The Messenger*, the magazine of the Apostleship of Prayer run by the Jesuits, began spreading the visions of St. Margaret Mary, declaring the only way France would be saved from her enemies was to embrace the devotion to the Sacred Heart. The message inspired Fr. de Boylesve. He became a chaplain to the Catholic Papal Zouaves forces sent to defend the French Motherland from the Protestant invaders, giving them rousing sermons: "Clotilde, inspiring faith in Clovis, saved the Franks and slaughtered the Germans at their feet ... Joan of Arc by her standard delivered France from the English! Your standard is the Sacred Heart." The Zouaves placed the Sacred Heart on their banner. Fr. de Boylesve also busily spread Sacred Heart badges of wool for the soldiers to pin on their uniforms, for they were in high demand. A gifted and inspiring preacher, his sermons encouraged them onward, even when they were driven back in defeat by the Prussians to where the soldiers remarked: "This man can lead us to the fire tomorrow; we would gladly be killed for him."

Fr. de Boylesve is fondly remembered today in Catholic circles in France for his work as the director of the Apostleship of Prayer in Le Mans through which he contributed to the spread of devotion to the Sacred Heart. On October 17, 1870 Fr de Boylesve was appointed to preach at the Visitation of Le Mans upon St. Margaret Mary for his subject, who at the time was a Blessed. He also preached upon another mystic who had died within their own times, Mother Marie de Jesus (1797-1854) from the convent des Oiseaux of

Paris who had received revelations from the Sacred Heart that were favourably recognised by the Archbishop of Paris. On June 21, 1823 the Sacred Heart revealed to Sr. Marie that He desired France be consecrated to His Sacred Heart by the King, and that a chapel be built and dedicated to Him, and the feast of the national consecration be formally celebrated every year. "After my sermon," recounts Fr. Boylesve, "the Mother Superior expressed to me her astonishment at my silence with regard to an almost similar order that Our Lord had given to Blessed Margaret Mary on June 17th, 1689. I confessed that in our college, which had barely opened for a month, I had not found the letters of the Blessed One and that I was unaware of the apparition and the order she was telling me about. I promised to make good this omission." Apparently at that time, the Sacred Heart's requests to St. Margaret Mary for a shrine and the national consecration of France by the King were not yet widely known.

True to his word, filled with his characteristic zeal for faith and country, doing what he could to extend the reign of Jesus Christ through his beloved homeland and secure its safety, the very next day he repaired his omission by publishing a pamphlet featuring the prophecies of St. Margaret Mary and Mother Marie de Jesus entitled "Triumph of France by the Sacred Heart", composing a special prayer of consecration to be said, which the Zouaves said every Friday as hope in the Sacred Heart was sorely needed. Paris was threatened with destruction by bombardments, then starvation by the invading Prussians, having commenced a siege around the city in September 1870. The siege continued until January 1871, the citizens reduced to dire circumstances. The zoo animals were slaughtered for food, the populace also living off of stray animals and rats. While the Prussian advance had ceased, humiliation still ensued when France suffered defeat at the hands of the Prussians with the establishment of the German Empire, also losing the territory of the Alsace-Lorraine to the victors. The troubles were not over. From March to May 1871 Paris fell into the clutches of the anticlerical socialist Communards, rebels revolting against the new government of the Third Republic. Blood ran in the streets, historical buildings burned, including the Tuileries Palace. The anticlerical Communards also executed the Archbishop of Paris, Georges Darboy, fulfilling the prophecy of St. Catherine Laboure. This horrific turn of events, combined with the circulation of prophecies foretelling the destruction of Paris was at hand, the faithful no doubt felt doom hung over the city. The times were desperate. After several reprintings, including a full reproduction of the text by Fr. Ramiere in the 'Messenger' newsletter issued by the Apostleship of Prayer, more than 330,000 copies of Fr. de Boylesve's pamphlets of the 'Triumph of the Sacred Heart' were circulated. It contributed to the rapid spread devotion to the Sacred Heart and bolstered the call to have the Universal Church consecrated to the Sacred Heart, also to build a national shrine on Montmartre in atonement for the atrocities committed by the Communards who began their uprising there. Construction began in 1875, the cornerstone was laid on June 16, 1875, the day Bl. Pius IX encouraged all the faithful to pray the consecration to the Sacred Heart using the special formula composed by the Sacred Congregation of Rites for the 200th anniversary of the apparition of the Sacred Heart to St. Margaret Mary. The construction of Sacre Coeur was at last completed in 1914.

As for Fr. Boylesve, in addition to his efforts to spread devotion to the Sacred Heart he worked unceasingly at many other endeavours, not only as director of the Apostolate of Prayer in Le Mans, but also with the Confraternities of Saint Joseph such as that of the Good Death, and also the Confraternity of the Agonizing Heart, the Work of Campaigns, Conferences of St. Vincent de Paul, Workers' Circles, he still appeared to dare all and sundry that they would never be able to find enough work for him to do. He amazed all that he was never at a loss for a subject to preach upon. He could easily vary his sermons to where it appeared he never preached the same way twice, and always captured his hearers' attention. One day out of curiosity a hardened sinner walked in to listen to him preach and left a converted man.

He also continued his prolific writing. One of his other well known works is "A Thought for Each Day of the Year", where it is evident his gift for giving interesting and encouraging sermons transferred to his pages. His meditations on the Gospels are crisp, clear, and easy to comprehend. They remain just as inspiring today as when they were penned well over a century ago.

When Fr. Boylesve wasn't working, he was praying. There was no question that he maintained a deep spiritual life. He was transferred to Vaugirard in 1875, returning to Le Mans two years later in 1877. Three years later his teaching came to an end at the college there with the decree of March 29, 1880 issued by the French minister for public education prohibiting the Jesuits from engaging in their educational apostolate, only the first of several anticlerical laws that would be passed in France over the next decades. Fr. Boylesve admitted he was on the verge of tears saying his last Mass for the students in the chapel before the school closed. Yet, he remained as active as ever despite this terrible blow, preaching, giving catechisms and continuing his writing, tackling the problems of their day threatening both the Church and society. He continued working despite his old age, until the end of 1891 when his activity was curtailed. He was struck with various ailments, first a tormenting dermatitis that remained with him, then inflammation of the blood that restricted his activities for many weeks, although he managed to say Mass and continue his writing, until at last he was struck with paralysis, unable to walk or speak. Clutching his rosary and his crucifix, the ever zealous 'priest-knight' of the Vendée gave up his soul to God in February 22, 1892 and was buried in the Jesuit cemetery of Sainte-Croix.[1]

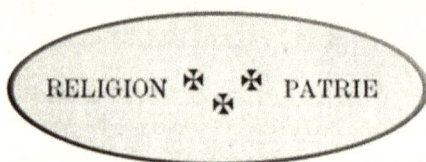

RELIGION ✠ ✠ ✠ PATRIE

---

1    Biographical information from 'Necrologie. Le Père Marin de Boylesve, in 'Lettres de Jersey', Vol.XII, No. 1 (April 1893)

# About this Edition

Fr. Marin de Boylesve's devotional book 'A Thought For Each Day of the Year' was translated into English by Wilfridus and originally published by the Catholic publishers Burns and Oates. This reprint is from the 1877 edition. While faithful to the original devotional text and its British spelling, this reprint features several changes and additions: a biography of the author has been added, the Table of Contents has been reconstructed, and dated punctuation such as extensive use of commas was amended where required for easier reading. Some older line art illustrations have been removed to allow for a larger print edition, and some informative footnotes have been added where needed.

## How to Keep Track of the Meditations

The mediations start at the beginning of the liturgical year, which is the First Sunday of Advent. Of course, there is no 'rule' saying you have to wait and start these mediations then, you may commence them any time. You need not even follow them in order if you wish, however, since Fr. Boylesve designed these daily reflections around the liturgical year, it is a practical way to keep your prayer life centred with the liturgical cycle of the Church.

As this book was written in the 1800s, it follows the Traditional Liturgical Calendar, which is used for the Latin Mass. If you attend the Latin Mass you should have no problems following along, especially if you have a daily missal.

If the old calendar is new to you, you will find certain Sundays are named differently and might be confusing as the number of Sundays after the Epiphany and Pentecost change each year depending on when Easter occurs, etc. The easiest way to keep track is to find a Traditional liturgical calendar online for the year you are making these meditations, they are not hard to find on the internet these days. Or, you can follow along with the Table of Contents here, which has been reconstructed with directions on what to do should there be extra Sundays after the Epiphany and / or Pentecost. If you lose track, search for certain days such as Ash Wednesday, Ascension Thursday, Corpus Christi, the Feast of the Sacred Heart, etc.. From these set feasts you can calculate where you are at or should be at in the calendar, and adjust your meditations accordingly.

NOTE: Fr. de Boylesve also made things interesting by including a second set of meditations for the week of Ascension Thursday. Therefore, if you plan to continue these meditations for more than one year, you can then vary them at this point so they do not seem 'stale' through repetition.

E.A. Bucchianeri

# Advent

## 1 ~ First Sunday in Advent

**"And there shall be signs in the sun, and in the moon, and in the stars."** ~ St. Luke **(21:25)**

**Thought**: Let us learn to read in the book of nature. God is always speaking to us there. The perfect regularity existing in the usual course of things shows forth the wisdom, kindness, and power of the Creator, and teaches us to observe the same regularity in our lives.

We should also learn a lesson from the accidents, and confusion, and apparent disorder which from time to time come upon us: the sudden fall of stars, earthquakes, inundations, famine, and pestilence all have some divine meaning, and we should look upon them as signs of justice coming from the avenging hand of the Lord, and we should take them to heart as solemn warnings.

**Prayer**: Jesus, grant that I may understand the signs of Thy coming, that I may foresee Thy just anger, and disarm it by prayer and mortification.

**Practice**: See and hear God everywhere and in all things.

ಐಐ❀ಲಚ

## 2 ~ Monday

**"Man withering away for fear and expectation of what shall come upon the whole earth."** ~ St. Luke (21:26)

**Thought:** God frightens us in order to save us. These formidable catastrophes which overpower nature itself are the direct work of His hand. It is the last supreme effort made by His mercy to convince the unbeliever, to convert the impious and to forewarn us of the rigour of justice. And at the end of the world these signs will be repeated, by means of which our Lord Jesus Christ will offer repentance to the wicked, presenting Himself for the last time as their Saviour before appearing as their Judge.

**Prayer:** Jesus, Thou strikest me with Thy hand of mercy, Thou castest down all that is around me, that I may withdraw myself from worldly things, that I may give my heart to the things of heaven. Thou wouldst raise me up, so that I may never fall again; Thou wouldst teach me to resist the torrent that carries so many poor souls away: Thou wouldst have me stand firm in the way of salvation. In Thy goodness Thou discoverest to me an imaginary hell here on earth that I may foresee the horror of the eternal reality.

**Practise:** Profit by the too real evils of this life, to separate yourself from all the attraction it may offer to your gaze.

கூஜ ✠ ஐஜ

## 3 ~ Tuesday

**"For the powers of heaven shall be moved."**
**~ St. Luke (21:26)**

**Thought:** In the material order of things, those bodies that we call attraction repulsion, gravitation, affinity, and cohesion will some day be suspended, and will at once cease to act; the stars and elements that they maintained in actual order will come in contact with one another, clash, and finally dissolve. ...
Thus is it in the moral order of things, the strongest minds hesitate in their faith and principles, men of most determined will and energy waver in their resolutions; hence at times a social chaos, worse by far than any material chaos.

**Prayer:** Jesus, guide me through this intellectual, social, moral chaos, which seems even now a prelude to the disorder of the Last Day.

**Practise:**   Put your trust in God, confiding in Him alone, thus being able to say, "Who shall separate us from the charity and love of Our Lord Jesus Christ?"

ಬುಜಾ ❈ ೧ಞೞ

## 4 ~ **Wednesday**

**"And they shall see the Son of man coming on a cloud with great power and majesty."** ~ St. Luke (26:27)

**Thought:**   Alas!  It will be too late for those who only begin to look up to Him then!  Yet He is always with us.   He is in heaven at the right hand of the Father, but He is also on our altars, in the tabernacle. A cloud of glory hides Him from us in the heavens; here on earth the symbol "bread" conceals His majesty from our sight, nevertheless He is here.  My Lord!  My Sovereign!  My Saviour and my Judge!  Thou art here! Unseen, Thou seest us one and all.  Thou seest me, and I shall have to render an account of all my thoughts, words and actions to Him.

**Prayer**:   Jesus, for the future I would walk in the ways of salvation; all my thoughts, words, and deeds shall tend to Thy service and to the greater glory of Thy name.

**Practise:** Have Jesus ever before your eyes, firstly as God, and secondly as Man – not in His body, which cannot be in all places at the same time, but by the eye of His majesty, which has already judged your actions, and has acquitted or condemned you.

ಬಾ಼ಾ಄಄ಡಿಐ಄

## 5 ~ Thursday

**"Look up, and lift your heads, because your redemption is at hand."**
**~ St. Luke (26: 28)**

**Thought**: Ye just, lift up your heads; those scourges, awful precursors of the final judgement, shall only frighten the impious. To you just men the hour of deliverance and redemption is at hand. You can look your persecutors boldly in the face, saying to them, "But a short while, and your turn will come. Triumph in your wickedness, despisers of all truth and justice! But hasten on your victory, for the morrow shall see truth avenged and justice done."

**Prayer**: Jesus, in Thee only do I confide! Thou art my support and strength. With Thee for Protector, I can despise the threats and anger of the powerful. They may tyrannise and oppress, load us with chains, banish us from our country, put us to death even, but Thou, O Lord, at last shalt conquer, and with Thee we also shall triumph.

**Practise:** Despise the world and all its threats.

ಬಾ಼ಾ಄಄ಡಿಐ಄

## 6 ~ Friday

**"This generation shall not pass away, until all things are fulfilled." ~ St. Luke (21:32)**

**Thought**:  Everything in the world tends to the Last Judgement; everything prepares the way for the defeat of Lucifer and his wicked followers, and the solemn triumph of Our Lord Jesus Christ and the good. It is for this reason that those partial judgements are sent which, being repeated during each generation, become dreadful warnings and shadows of the Last and General Judgement.  The Deluge, the burning of Sodom, the feast of Balthasar, those revolutions against society and state, all those sudden and terrible changes which strike down now a single family, now a whole nation, are only examples of what will be seen at the Last Day.

**Prayer**: Jesus, grant me knowledge and docility to understand and profit by the warnings of Thy justice and mercy.

**Practice:**  You must not be scandalised at the triumph of the wicked; the day is not far off when you shall see justice done to both.

ဃ၁၈ဝ❀ఴంఴ

# 7 ~ Saturday

**"Heaven and earth shall pass away, but My word shall not pass away."**

**~ St. Luke (21:32)**

**Thought:** Wherefore should I fix my mind on passing things? The earth whose soil I tread turns upon its axis and moves round the sun; the sun itself and all the starry bodies whirl round one another, and around some unknown centre. In the midst of this continual revolution one thing alone, ... the word of Jesus Christ is firm and settled! All things pass and disappear – nothing remains firm, nothing ever returns! Time, fortune, pleasure, honour, speech, and human thought – all, all are lost. No; all that has been thought, spoken, or desired in honour or in the service of Him whose word never passes away, ... is remembered and retained.

**Prayer:** Jesus, Thou shalt be the only object of my love, the never-changing centre of all my thoughts and actions.

**Practise:** Think, speak, work, and live for Jesus only.

৩০৪৩ ✤ ৫৫৬৪

ଓଞ୍ଚ❀ଓଓଞ୍ଚ❀ଓଓ

## 8 ~ Second Sunday in Advent

**"Art Thou He that art to come, or look we for another?"** ~ St. Matthew (11:3)

**Thought:** Our mission is like that of John the Baptist, viz., to announce the coming of Jesus Christ, and to prepare the way for Him. As soon as He comes, our work is done. What matter it if we are left in the power of our persecutors, if only Christ be recognised and known? Those Christians who are able, and yet refuse to help those engaged in preaching the advent of Our Lord, are cowardly and ungrateful.

**Prayer:** Jesus, Thou art He that art to come. The world by its crimes retarded Thy coming for four thousand years. I by my faults hinder Thy coming to me, and to others.

**Practise:** Forget yourself entirely, for Jesus Christ.

ଞ୍ଚ❀ଓଓ

## 9 ~ Monday

**"The blind see, the dead rise, the poor have the gospel preached to them."**
~ St. Matthew (11:5)

**Thought:** Jesus gives proof of His mission and of His Divinity by His omnipotence and His bounty – His omnipotence attested by His miracles, His bounty acknowledged by the person whom He cures. Let us admire this gradual progress. Jesus, after making known the most wonderful of miracles, viz., the raising of the dead to life, makes known a miracle still more wonderful, the preaching of the Gospel to the poor. Jesus proclaims the Divinity of the Church by its instruction of the poor in the simple catechism of religion. Human pride does not condescend to lower itself to the poor of this world, unless perhaps to corrupt them, or raise them in sedition.

**Prayer:** Jesus, grant me the privilege of helping Thee in preaching the Gospel to the poor.

**Practise:** It is always in your power to help and comfort the poor. Do not forget, in extending a hand of relief to their corporal wants, to offer them spiritual help and comfort.

༺ꗬ❀ꗬ༻

## 10 ~ Tuesday

**"And blessed is he that shall not be scandalised in Me." ~ St. Matthew (6:6)**

**Thought:** This is another sign of the Divine mission, I mean the contradiction that one meets with when doing the work of the Lord, for in doing His work you put yourself in direct opposition to the sinner. Your work stands as an obstacle to his work; your word is a contradiction of his word; your conduct condemns his conduct. From which we are to conclude that either he will reform and you will be the means of saving him, or, he remaining stubborn in his own will, must perish miserably.

**Prayer:** Jesus, ought I to be ashamed of fighting in holy warfare when Thou hast so courageously led the way? Man has done all in his power to prevent Thee from doing good, from saving souls; must I then wonder that they should try their utmost to overthrow my good designs either by the refusal of their co-operation or by their deadly opposition?

**Practice:** Be not discouraged at the sight of the inactivity of your fellow Catholics or the persecution of the wicked.

ಜಞ🏵ಲಚ

### 11 ~ Wednesday

**"What went you out into the desert to see? A reed shaken with the wind?"**
**~ St. Matthew (6:7)**

**Thought:** Constancy is the first thing necessary to the just man, it is the first step towards holiness. Constancy is a firm resolution, an unalterable determination to always pursue the object we have in view, and on no account to be ever discouraged or disconcerted. It should surmount all difficulties, bearing up against tribulation and persecution, conquering passion. Come what may, the just man remains immovable. The saint is ever the same, everything may change around him, but he will stand alone sooner than yield to the storm. Like the mountains which tower so proudly above the earth, like the rocks against which the winds and waves may break in fury without shaking their foundation in the least, so will his views remain unshaken and his will remain firm in spite of all that the crowd may do to make it waver.

**Prayer:** O Jesus! In the midst of this changeable world where can I find the invincible strength of will and purpose necessary for doing good? In Thee, in Thee only, O Lord. Thou art infallible Truth, immutable Holiness.

**Practise:** Listen to the words of Jesus by faith and good intention, and endeavour to imitate His conduct by charity.

ಓಜಾ ❀ ಲಾ೦ಚ

### 12 ~ Thursday

**"But what went you out to see?  A man clothed in soft garments?"**
~ **St. Matthew (11:8)**

**Thought:** The effeminate dress of courtiers is generally a sign of a sensual and worldly life. The just

47

man is dressed simply, his whole demeanour is modest. Not only the life he leads but the very sight of him is a condemnation of those men of pampered tastes, those lovers of luxury. And what are they? But too often the humble servants of some one greater than themselves, who in turn is slave and servant to his passions, or else is governed ignominiously by his ministers or his favourites.

**Prayer:** Jesus, may I ever hate and despise the effeminate sensual life of worldly people; draw me closer to Thy cross, which is the only true and glorious ornament of a Christian.

**Practise:** Be simple, yet resolute, in your thoughts, words, and actions.

ಬಙ⊛ಲ೮ಟ

## 13 ~ Friday

"But what went you out to see? A prophet? Yea, I tell you, more than a prophet."<br>~ St. Matthew (11:9)

**Thought:** Separated from the world rather by interior solitude than by exterior solitude, the just man no longer judges things or persons according as the world judges them, but by means of the double light which he has received from God – by means of reason and faith. Judging by means of reason, he is man, he is wise, he is just; by means of faith, he is a Christian, he is holy, he is a prophet, and more than a prophet –

prophet, for the future is revealed to him by faith, which promises him sight of God in glory; more than a prophet, for without touching on the future he already sees the Hand and Presence of God where another sees only the hand of man or the result of chance; just as St. John the Baptist distinguished Our Lord as Saviour, whilst the people took Him to be one, mortal like themselves. Through faith, then, the Christian sees God in all things, even in His humbling Himself and suffering for us upon the cross.

**Prayer:** Jesus, make me to feel that Thou art present, contriving everything that may tend to my perfection in this life and my happiness in the next.

**Practise:** Bless the Lord at all times, but more especially in times of trial and affliction.


ಜುಜು ✤ ಲ಼ುಲ಼

### 14 ~ Saturday

**"Behold, I send My angel before Thy face, who shall prepare Thy way before Thee."**
**~ St. Matthew (11:10)**

**Thought:** This is what we also have to do. Every Christian is sent to prepare the way for Jesus Christ, though it is more especially the duty of those consecrated to God. Let us look back and see how St. John the Baptist fulfilled this glorious work. Not only did he astonish the world by the sanctity and mortification of his life, and by his contempt of all worldly honour, but he also showed the rich the folly of their ways of life, and opened their eyes to the vice into which they had fallen. The Pharisees and courtiers, the publicans and sinners, soldiers and magistrates, all heard the condemnation of their conduct pronounced by this zealous and intrepid precursor of Our Lord.

**Prayer:** Jesus, give me knowledge and courage to prepare the hearts of my fellow creatures to receive Thy Divine and kingly rule.

**Practise:** Have but one thought, but one wish, viz., that Jesus may reign over all hearts.

ಖುಖಿ ✿ ಲ೪ುಖಖುಖಿ ✿ ಲ೪ುಖಖುಖಿ ✿ ಲ೪ು

## 15 ~ Third Sunday of Advent

### "Who art thou?" ~ St. John (1: 19)

**Thought:** John the Baptist lived a lonely and mortified life in the desert. It was not necessary for him to show himself to become known. No; the more you try to fly the world and all its pleasures and deceits, the more you will find it desirous of knowing and admiring you, and in its wonder at your conduct it will say to you, *Tu quis es?* "Who art thou?" Alas! The world might ask us, though in a far different sense; "Christian, who art though? Minister of God, who art thou? Monk or religious, who art thou?" Judging from our actions, the world would take us for pagans or worldlings, but never for Christians. Let us not astonish the world by the contrast of our conduct with what we profess to do; let us rather contrast their

50

conduct and maxims with our good principle and honest way of life.

**Prayer:** Jesus, give me grace so to imitate Thy virtues as to be mistaken, like Thy precursor, St. John the Baptist.

**Practice:** Make an open profession of your faith in all things.

ಬಿಞ⊕ಞಲ

## 16 ~ Monday

**"And he confessed, and did not deny; and he confessed; I am not the Christ."**
**~ St. John (1: 20)**

**Thought:** John refused a name not his own: we, alas! Too often refuse what is ours by right of baptism. We blush to acknowledge who we are and to appear as we should, as Catholics. St. John feared not to forfeit the popularity of the world in declaring that he was not the Christ; but we fear to lose our position, to compromise our interests or the chance of advancement, in making open avowal of our faith.

**Prayer:** O Jesus! May I never blush acknowledge Thee as my Saviour; my I never be ashamed of Thy Cross, Thus Gospel, or Thy holy Church.

**Practise:** Prove yourself a Christian by your action, but without human respect or ostentation.

ಖಿಜಿ �֎ ಲ৪౬౪

## 17 ~ Tuesday

**"What then? Art thou Elias? And He said: I am not." ~ St. John (1:21)**

**Thought:** Our manner of life should be such that we may be known as servants of God; but we should not try to pass for what we are not. St John tells the Jews that he is not Elias. He who humbles himself shall be exalted. Our Lord declares that he is Elias; and if he be not really Elias in body, we may almost say that the sanctity of his life and the importance of his mission makes him greater than Elias. He resembles Elias in his rude, austere way of living; and as from Elias bursts forth impressive eloquence, startling, striking as the lightning, so does it burst from St. John the Baptist. His mission is higher even than that of Elias. He is sent to announce the coming of Our Lord.

**Prayer:** O Jesus! Like John the Baptist, I will live to announce the salvation which Thou offerest to mankind; and like Elias, I will foretell the Last Day when Thou wilt descend to judge all men.

**Practise:** Let Jesus be the principal and entire object of your thoughts, words and deeds.

ಖಿಜಿ ✖ ಲ৪౬౪

# 18 ~ Wednesday

## "What sayest thou of thyself."
### ~ St. John (1:22)

**Thought:** Nothing is grander or nobler than a truthful man! Nothing more rare! Who will dare to say that he is such? There is always something within us that we are anxious to hide. It is easy to believe that man should wish to conceal his faults – natural pride prompts him to it; but what is strange, indeed, is, that we should appear more ashamed of our virtues and our good actions than of our vices and our bad deeds. A Catholic is ashamed to own his religion, to appear Catholic in word and deed by observing the commandments and by frequenting the sacraments, whilst the libertine glories in his debaucheries.

**Prayer:** Jesus, if I am ashamed to call myself Thy disciple, Thou wilt blush to call Thyself my Master. If I disown Thy Name and Thy Cross, Thou wilt disown me in my cowardice and weakness. Give me courage to feel and act as becomes a Catholic.

**Practise:** Pay no heed to the contempt and sneers of this world.

బుకు✸యుక

## 19 ~ Thursday

**"I am the voice of one crying in the wilderness, Make straight the way of the Lord."**
**~ St. John (1:23)**

**Thought:** How humble, and yet how sublime! I am but a voice, meaning, in myself I am nought. What is the voice left to itself? It is but a vain sound; but here it is animated and guided in its course by God Himself. John is, then, the voice of God. In humbling himself he is exalted.

**Prayer:** Jesus, grant me to be as Thy voice, and to be only Thine. May I speak only with the view of preparing the hearts and minds of others to receive the gifts of faith and grace.

**Practise:** Make it a rule to speak of Jesus or in His honour. If, as St. Paul says, all our actions – even the meals we take – can be done for the greater glory of God how much more honour can be rendered by our words and good example?

శుభ❀రాత్రి

## 20 ~ Friday

**"There hath stood one in the midst of you, whom you know not." ~ St. John (1:26)**

**Thought:** This Unknown One is still in the midst of us. Alas! He is still unknown. Nowadays, infidels – that is, the greater part of mankind – know Him not. Protestants refuse to believe His Real Presence in the sacraments of His love. Schismatics will not recognise them in the person of His Vicar here on earth. Catholics forget Him, or offend Him so much, that one would think they did not believe in Him at all. There are many who by their position in the world should live solely for Him and by Him, I mean monks and religious of different orders; how many of these are there not who scarcely think of Him, even during the short hours they are supposed to pass at the foot of the altar?

**Prayer:** Jesus, grant that I may be different from the crowd of persons who coldly pass Thee by, slighting Thee, and showing Thee such indifference!

**Practise:** Remember always that you live, act, and combat under the eye of Jesus, your King and Judge.

ಜಜಾ ⊕ ಲಜ೦ಜ

## 21 ~ Saturday

**"The latchet of whose shoe I am not worthy to loose." ~ St. John (1:27)**

**Thought:** If St. John the Baptist is not worthy to loose the latchet of a shoe upon the foot of Jesus Christ, how unworthy then am I to partake in great undertakings, such as preaching His Gospel, and above all, receiving Him in the Holy Eucharist. I should be too highly honoured in having confided to me the humblest employment in the service of the Church, I should be happy in the very last ranks of the Catholic army. The least service rendered to Jesus Christ is worth far more than the highest dignity of the State.

**Prayer:** Jesus, Thou hast no need of my services, permit me, nevertheless, to do something in Thy honour, not with the hopes of praise and merited applause, but to prove my love for Thee.

**Practise:** Honour and serve Our Lord in the person of your fellow creatures, in rendering them every little service in your power.

ಙೞ⊕ಲಚ

## 22 ~ Fourth Sunday of Advent

**"The word of the Lord was made known unto John the son of Zachary in the desert."**
**~ St. Luke (3:2)**

**Thought:** Jesus speaks in the wilderness; it is there, in the solitude and in silence, that He speaks to us either by secret inspiration, or by the mouth of our superiors. The world is governed by men who are separated from the world, free of will and action; for a king never mixes among the crowd, he keeps apart, alone, and at a distance, showing himself but rarely to his people, and only on grand occasions and in times of peril and difficulty. To govern well or give sound judgement, we should hold aloof and look on things from a distance.

**Prayer:** Jesus, I await the sound of Thy voice. Perhaps Thou hast already spoken to me, but such has been the noise and din around me that I have heard nothing. I will seek Thee in the wilderness, where all is tranquil and undisturbed.

**Practise:** Prepare a solitude within your heart, and Jesus will speak to you there, and will make known His word.

ಬಜ⊛ಞಬಜ

## 23 ~ Monday

"And he came into all the country about the Jordan, preaching the baptism of penance for the remission of sins." ~ St. Luke (3:3)

**Thought:** Remain in solitude until God calls you from it – that is to say, until your duty compels you to leave it in order to fulfil the obligation of charity or propriety. And when again in public, preach by word if you are authorised to do so, and by examples if such be not your duty: preach purification (*baptismum*), for the world is but soil and stain; and penance (*poenitentia*), for it is but sin.

**Prayer:** O Jesus! Grant that my only ambition may be to make Thee better known and loved by men.

**Practice:** Do not let one single day pass without doing something for the glory of Jesus.

ಜಜ⊛ಡಣ

## 24 ~ Tuesday

"A voice of one crying in the wilderness."
~ St. Luke (3:4)

**Thought:** Let us cry out and speak boldly of the Lord, even in the desert, when those around us refuse to listen or pretend not to understand. Our intellect and the power of speech are given to us solely that we may praise the Lord and make others praise Him. It is not for us to say that success shall crown our efforts; all that we have to do is to speak, to make the effort. But I am alone! There is none to hear me! Persevere, nevertheless, and like to St. John the Baptist, you will soon be surrounded by the crowd.

**Prayer:** Jesus, may I ever echo Thy praises; may I ever help in that most important work, the redemption of the world, by invoking Thy Holy Name and by preaching Thy doctrine.

**Practise:** Speak of God in the desert, even when abandoned, when completely isolated from the rest of mankind. A single word is enough to obtain a conversion or to forward some good work.

ಋಙ❀ಚೞ

## 25 ~ Wednesday

**"Prepare ye the way of the Lord, make straight His paths."** ~ St. Luke (3:4)

**Thought:** Jesus is desirous of entering into our souls. The road that should lead Him towards us is our goodwill, and the pathway by which He may penetrate into the depths of our souls is holy desire and upright intention. Let us then clear the way of all obstacles, casting from our minds all irregular affections, smoothing and mending the paths, for when the road is long and winding it is easy to lose one's self. Above all, let us firmly recall our desires and intentions, no longer allowing them to wander away from God, nor suffering them to linger or lose themselves in the seductive maze of worldly delight.

**Prayer**: Jesus, grant that Thy glory may be the only object of my words and actions, that they may have no other rule than Thy Holy Will.

**Practise:** Constantly renew and purify your intentions.

౪౸ఁ❀ఁ౻౦

## 26 ~ Thursday

**"Every valley shall be filled; and every mountain and hill shall be brought low."**
**~ St. Luke (3:5)**

**Thought:** The valleys are meant to represent low, sensual, and worldly inclinations; the mountains are types of pride, and the hills represent vanity. Are you longing for Jesus to enter into your heart? Raise up your inclinations, thoughts, desires; cast off from you all that is earthy and unclean; rise out of the quagmires of sensuality and cupidity. At the same time, do not forget to lower your pride and your pretensions to vanity; in a word, be straightforward and simple.

**Prayer:** Jesus, give me strength to resist the fascination that would draw me towards the things of earth and towards sensual pleasure, give me strength to resist the outbursts of pride and the swell of vanity.

**Practise:** Walk evenly and regularly in the path of perfection, without being discouraged or cast down, and without being raised up with presumption.

☜☞✵❧☙

## 27 ~ Friday

**"And the crooked (paths) shall be made straight, and the rough ways plain."**
~ St. Luke (3:5)

**Thought:** Rectify your intentions, moderate your passions, repress all excess, correct yourself of your faults. Are you given to impatience, acquire sweetness of disposition. Are you lazy and neglectful, stir yourself to activity. Are all your thoughts centred in self, do you seek self in everything, then forget self in order to think only of the glory of God, interest yourself in Him and in His creatures.

**Prayer:** Jesus, show me in what I must correct myself, likewise strengthen in me the resolution of combating my faults.

**Practise:** Select one particular failing, and pursue it without ceasing until you have completely conquered it.

☜☞✵❧☙

## 28 ~ Saturday

**"And all flesh shall see the salvation of the Lord." ~ St. Luke (3:6)**

**Thought:** God deigns to make Himself visible to save us. Not only does He take a soul like ours, but He also clothes Himself in flesh like to our flesh. And strange to say, there are men calling themselves Christians who acknowledge His power in great things, yet dispute it in little things. They will allow Him to be the Master of their souls, but not the king of their bodies. They grant the Church power in spiritual matters, but in refuse it any voice in temporal and material affairs, as though time were not subject to eternity, the material to the spiritual, as if the Word had not taken a body as well as a soul.

**Prayer:** Jesus, extend Thy reign over my body and its senses, as well as over my soul and its powers; command me not only as a Christian, but also as a citizen and as a man. Thou art King of the worldly empire as Thou art King of the spiritual.

**Practise:** Subordinate the body to the mind, the worldly man to the religious, Caesar to Christ, and in time of combat exclaim, "It is better to obey God than man."

ೞಞ❀ಚಚೞ

ಖಞ❀ಝೞಖಞ❀ಝೞಖಞ❀ಝೞ

## Christmas Time

ಖಞ❀ಝೞಖಞ❀ಝೞಖಞ❀ಝೞ

## 29 ~ Sunday (Christmas Day / Season)

"And Joseph also went up ... to be enrolled with Mary, his espoused wife, who was with child." ~ St. Luke (2: 4-5)

**Thought:** We here see the King of kings before His birth obeying a king of earth. Augustus, however, whilst sending forth his edicts to the utmost limits of the East, little knew that on his part he was obeying the decrees of the King of kings. God had foretold that the Saviour should be born in Bethlehem. In order that this might be accomplished He made use of Augustus, and through this prince the order was given for the census of the whole people. At the sight of those wars and revolutions that upset the world you feel inclined to imagine that God no longer governs the world or those in it. You are mistaken. God permits that these awful catastrophes should take place, just for the salvation and perfection of this or that person whom the world knows not.

**Prayer:** Jesus, like to Thee, I will be guided by Thy Providence, knowing that those who are over me are only Thy instruments.

**Practise:** Acknowledge Divine Providence in all things.

## 30 ~ Monday

**"And she brought forth her first-born son." ~ St. Luke (2:7)**

**Thought:** Behold Him who shall crush the head of the serpent, who shall be blessed by all nations and tribes of the earth; Him, the expected One of nations for four thousand years; behold, like to Moses the prophet, but greater than Moses, the Star of Jacob, the occupant of the throne of David whose sway shall stretch from sea to sea; behold Him carrying the world upon His shoulder; He is the loosened stone of the mountain which, after overthrowing the great powers of this world, shall rise up, forming itself into a great mountain, looking down upon the whole world. This is He, superior to all – and yet how little is He. The Angel said that He should be *great*. "He shall be great." "*Hic erit magnus*;" but He is a little child who is now given to us! *Parvulum datus est nobis.*

**Prayer:** O infant Jesus! Thou art as great and powerful in Thy stable as when seated on the right hand of Thy Father in heaven.

**Practise:** Never judge by appearances.

ಞಞ❀ಞಞ

## 31 ~ Tuesday

### "And she laid Him in a manger."
### ~ St. Luke (11:7)

**Thought:** And she laid Him in a manger! A manger! Behold the cradle, the throne of the Son of man, of the Son of God! And yet a Christian would esteem and seek for riches, comfort, honour! *Hic erit magnus!* This Child shall be great, or, rather, is the only Great One. The poor are therefore greater than the rich; the sufferer is greater than the man of ease and comfort; he that is despised by the world is greater than he whom the world honours; and in truth, riches make slaves of us, pleasure softens and corrupts us, and honour is only paid to those who sell themselves to obtain it. Let us seat ourselves at the humblest place, living a severe life, not looking after worldly goods; then we shall be free and great like the Infant God.

**Prayer:** Jesus, Thou art poor, suffering, and despised, but I adore Thee; I would be poor with Thee, partaking of Thy sufferings and sharing the contempt that is shown Thee.

**Practice:** Sacrifice each day something that the world esteems and seeks for with such unworthy zeal.

ജ‍ഇ❀ഉങ

## 32 ~ Wednesday

**"Behold I bring you tidings of great joy."**
**~ St. Luke (2:10)**

**Thought:** What have these shepherds done that they should be the first called to the crib of the Infant God? They were simple and poor, but there were many others like to them in poverty and simplicity. Why then were these preferred? They were at their posts, watching and guarding their flocks. Be you always at your post. However humble, however rough may be your occupation, if you fulfil your duty with obedience, God, seeing you thus employed, will fill your heart with joy and enlighten your mind when you least expect it.

**Prayer:** Jesus, Thou alone art the joy of my soul, in Thee alone can I find safety. Thou art the light of the intelligence and the giver of strength to the will.

**Practise:** Fulfil your duty, no matter what may happen; nothing will happen that God does not ordain.

ജ‍ഇ❀ഉങ

## 33 ~ Thursday

"And this shall be a sign unto you. You shall find the Infant wrapped in swaddling-clothes, and laid in a manger." ~ St. Luke (2:12)

**Thought:** How are we to recognise by this sign a God, a Saviour? God is majesty, glory, and power. The Saviour is the emblem of strength and courage. And so it is. Oh, admire majesty, glory, and power in this Child! Wrapped in swaddling-clothes, He has but a manger for His throne and altar, and yet the heavens are moved, the Angels sing of Him as the glory of the Most High, as the Saviour of the world. If He clothes Himself with weakness, it is in order that by that very weakness He may save souls and defeat the enemy.

**Prayer:** Jesus, unite my weakness to Thine, and that, together with Thy Divine Strength, will be stronger than all the power of earth and hell.

**Practise:** Place your trust in God alone.

೮ಐ⊕ ೞಅ

## 34 ~ Friday

"Glory to God in the highest, and on earth peace to men of good will." ~ St. Luke (2:14)

**Thought:** Glory to God!  From this Child bursts forth the wisdom, bounty, and power of the Most High. Wisdom, inasmuch as He could find no better way of winning our hearts than by taking upon Himself our humanity and becoming a babe like each of us. Bounty, for what greater proof could He give us of His love, than by making Himself *one* of us.   Power, for as a feeble child He attracts to His dwelling kings and shepherds, and makes the powerful of this world tremble at His name. What, then, will He be when He shows Himself in the splendour of His strength.

**Prayer:**  Jesus, grant me the good will of the shepherds and the Magi, who, to follow the first heavenly inspiration, left these their flocks, those their kingdoms.

**Practise:** Listen with promptness and docility to the call of grace.

ಐಓ✹ಲ೪

## 35 ~ Saturday

**"And they found Mary and Joseph, and the Infant lying in the manger."**
**~ St. Luke (2:16)**

**Thought:** The manger is the sign by which we are to recognise the God Infant, the God King, the God Saviour.  Being God, He would conquer all that the world holds most invincible by making Himself  most feeble, knowing that His Strength and Power lies in His very weakness. Being King, He rules the land without the magnificence of a court or the splendour of an army. Being Saviour, He shows us that He is free from all those chins which fetter us like slaves, viz., riches, pleasures, honour.

**Prayer:** Jesus, I conjure Thee by the remembrance of the manger, to teach me to esteem all that this world despises, and to despise all that it esteems.

**Practise:** You are despised! You suffer – you are in want of something! Rejoice, then, for in this you are like to the Infant Jesus.

ಜಞ✿ಚಾಚಜಞ✿ಚಾಚಜಞ✿ಚಾಚ

## 36 ~ Sunday After Christmas Day

**"And the father and mother were wondering at those things which were spoken concerning Him." ~ St. Luke (2:33)**

**Thought:** They knew a great deal more about Him than those who spoke about Him; but they were glad to hear the greatness of the Divine Child spoken of. Let us, like Joseph and Mary, hide in secrecy the lights that we have received, but let us rejoice to hear others praise Our Lord, and celebrate His greatness.

**Prayer:** Jesus, if Thou dost not think me worthy of preaching Thy kingdom, but wouldst have me silent, I will at least praise those who have received the gift of making Thee known and loved.

**Practise:** Rejoice at seeing Our Lord better praised and served by others than by yourself.

ಐಜಿ✠ಲೇಡ

## 37 ~ Monday

**"Behold this Child is set for the fall, and for the resurrection of many in Israel."**
**~ St. Luke (2:34)**

**Thought:** Jesus is King, and as such, lays claim to His Throne. Of mankind, some flock round His standard; to them He restores a life lost by sin, and assures them their eternal happiness – *Positus est hic in resurrectionem multorm*; others rise up against Him, but He is bound to reign, and if need be, must strike down all His enemies – *Positus est hic in ruinam multorum*.

**Prayer:** Jesus, be to me the Resurrection and the Life; by faith and grace strike down all that is of "self" in me.

**Practise:** Love Jesus only, and reject and combat all that is not to His honour.

ಐಜಿ✠ಲೇಡ

# 38 ~ Tuesday

**"And (He is set up) for a sign which shall be contradicted."** ~ St. Luke (2:34)

**Thought:** If you try to do or say anything for the glory of God and the salvation of souls, you will at once serve as a target for all sorts of contradiction. Passion and wrong that you would condemn and repress by word and action, rise up to stifle your voice and to overthrow your good work, and then the good, frightened by the impudence of the wicked, will unite among themselves to put a stop to what they will call *imprudence* on your part. Do not be disconcerted. Jesus was persecuted by every enemy of God and man, and abandoned by all save His mother, some few holy women, and one man, St. John, who alone followed Him to the cross.

**Prayer:** Jesus, sustain me in the day of persecution. I may be strong enough to combat the attacks of Thy enemies; but if abandoned by those calling themselves Thy friends, I shall fail unless Thou aidest me.

**Practise:** In the days of trial look to Jesus and Mary, and to them only for support and help.

ಬಙ❀ಞಚ

## 39 ~ Wednesday

**"And thy own soul a sword shall pierce."**
**~ St. Luke (2:35)**

**Thought:** The soul of Mary was pierced with a sword of sorrow; why then should I murmur at the suffering that I may have to undergo? Mary witnessed the abrupt ending of her Son's life in the midst of a career crowned with glory. All at once the cross changes His glory into ignominy and pain. Mary is powerless, she cannot help Him – she can only suffer.

**Prayer:** Jesus, if I could only suffer as Mary did at the sight of Thee humbled and in pain, but I can hardly bear the little bodily suffering that I am subject to. When shall I forget myself so entirely as to think only of Thy interests O Jesus! Interest which should be mine, and which alone should have any importance in my eyes?

**Practice:** Offer up each day's sufferings in unison with the Heart of Mary, that Heart so deeply pierced by the sword of sorrow.

ಚುಚು✿ಞಞ

## 40 ~ Thursday

**"And there was one Anna, a prophetess, ...**
**and she spoke of Him." ~ St. Luke (36:38)**

**Thought:** The gift of preaching the Word of God is only acquired by prayer and mortification and patience. Anna never departed from the temple, but prayed and fasted incessantly. It was only after eighty years that she saw the Lord and was allowed to speak of Him. Be patient, the light will show forth, and the word of the Lord will be given to you when you think there is no longer any hope.

**Prayer:** Jesus, I have been long waiting for *Thee*, I desire to do something for Thy glory. Thou wilt not disappoint me in my wish?

**Practise:** Never despair, and never say to yourself, Oh, it is too late!

ఙఙ❀ఛ౮

## 41 ~ Friday

**"And after they had performed all things according to the law of the Lord."**
~ St. Luke (2:39)

**Thought:** Never leave your *solitude* save to fulfil your duty, and when you have fulfilled it, return again to your retreat; but take care to do all that God wills and to do it perfectly. *Perfecerunt omnia.* Do not follow your own thoughts or ideas, but follow the law of God the rule of your state of life, and the orders of your superiors: *secundum legem Domini.*

**Prayer:** Jesus, grant that my sole satisfaction here on earth may be the knowledge that I have accomplished Thy will, that I have observed with regularity and good order the divers duties that my profession or situation may demand of me.

**Practise**: Be regular in everything you do.

ಬಞ⊛ಞಚ

## 42 ~ Saturday

**"And the Child grew and waxed strong, full of wisdom; and the grace of God was in Him." ~ St. Luke (2:40)**

**Thought:** You must not expect to attain perfection all at once. Jesus, who was the type of perfection, full of wisdom and grace from the moment of His Incarnation, *grew* and waxed strong. Little by little He disclosed the perfections hidden within His soul. Always strive to do your best according to the grace and strength that is given you; never turn back, always advance, but do not expect to gain the heights in one single bound.

**Prayer:** Jesus, grow strong in me, strengthen Thyself in me, and I shall then increase in virtue and wisdom as in years, both before God and man.

**Practise:** *Age quod agis*, whatever you do, do well, and for God alone. In this consists true and real perfection.

## 43 ~ Sunday After The Circumcision

"And after the Magi were departed, behold an angel of the Lord appeared in sleep to Joseph." ~ St. Matthew (2:13)

**Thought:** Joseph and Mary were pondering with feelings of pleasure over the homage rendered to the Divine Child by the angels and the Wise Men of the East, when behold, quite unexpectedly, an Angel appeared to Joseph in his sleep warning him of the peril that menaced the Child. Thus after day comes night, thus consolation follows trial. Here on earth, consolation is only granted to make us more ready for the fight.

**Prayer:** Jesus, dwell Thou in me, and I in Thee; for then nothing can trouble or afflict me.

**Practise:** Have confidence in God alone, look to Him for rest and comfort.

## 44 ~ Monday

**"Arise, and take the Child and His mother, and fly into Egypt."**
**~ St. Matthew (2:13)**

**Thought:** The Saviour needs a saviour!  A God flies!* Is not the thought enough to stagger our reason? Our Lord and Saviour could by one single word annihilate His enemies.  But if He triumphs through flight, and gains the throne by ways which are generally the means of forfeiting it, if, *in fine*, His very weakness is stronger than all human power, will you not recognise your God and Saviour?

**Prayer:** Jesus, Thou waitest until my weakness is proved, that then Thou mayest use me for the manifestation of Thy glory.

**Practise:** Trust in God, no matter what happens.

ಬಙ⊕ಲಚ

## 45 ~ Tuesday

**"And be there until I shall tell you."**
**~ St. Matthew (2:13)**

**Thought:** In this case the vagueness of the command is of itself enough to cause alarm.  Joseph must go into an unknown country, and reside there unknown to all.  Let us take courage and always

---

\*   To 'fly'-the old expression for 'flee'.

advance; the future may be hidden to us, but God knows it, and that is sufficient. God is wise and He has ordained all things beforehand. God is good and He has ordered everything for our good. God is all-powerful and all that He has ordained will take place; nothing can happen without His permission. No matter what happeneth, the end will be to His glory and for our happiness.

**Prayer:** Jesus, in Thy company I will look to the future without anxiety. With Thee nothing disastrous can ever come to pass.

**Practise**: Trust in God.

ಜುಙಿ✾ಞ಄

## 46 ~ Wednesday

**"For it will come to pass that Herod will seek the Child to destroy Him."**
**~ St. Matthew (2:13)**

**Thought:** Herod is still seeking the Child Jesus; the world still seeks the Child Jesus; in His mystical Body, the Church. Herod seeks the Church, not with the view of submitting to its authority and becoming one of its members, but to destroy it. This is why he watches and makes researches. Herod will not succeed; he may shed blood and make martyrs, but the Church shall escape his fury and survive – he will pass away, leaving nothing to posterity but the history of his crimes.

**Prayer:** Jesus, Thou Child and fugitive, art more powerful than Herod and all the heirs to his jealous anger; I will attach myself to Thy service, I will despise Herod.

**Practise:** Fear nothing that the world may say or do.

ೞಙ⊕ಚಚ

## 47 ~ Thursday

**"And Joseph arose and took the Child and His mother by night and retired into Egypt."**
**~ St. Matthew (2:14)**

**Thought:** The secret of wisdom and strength is a speedy and faithful obedience to the commands of our superiors. You are *wise* by prompt and faithful obedience inasmuch as you conform your intelligence to the Divine Intelligence of God; you become *wise* of the Wisdom of God Himself; you are *strong* by prompt and faithful obedience, for you conform your will to the Divine Will, you acquire goodness from the Goodness of God Himself, and power from His Power. But it is night and dark you will say. Obey, and God will be to you a light. But I shall have to go into Egypt! Obey God will be your help and strength, He will assist you against the impious and worldly persons who surround you.

**Prayer:** Jesus, Thou wilt be to me the only True Wisdom, the only real strength.

**Practise:** Obey at once without inquiring into reasons.

ಖಖ⊕ಞಞ

## 48 ~ Friday

**"And He was there (in Egypt) until the death of Herod." ~ St. Matthew (2:14)**

**Thought:** Stay in Egypt – that is, remain powerless – until the death of Herod. Herod will die; and with him will disappear the obstacle to the designs that you have conceived for the glory of God and the salvation of souls. But when is this to be? There lies the trial. May I not die before the realisation of my design? What does it matter, for after all, what are your desires? Are they for God's glory or your own? If for yours, it were better that you should die before the realisation of a project whose result would cause you pride, and which, far from gaining you the merits of heaven, would only tend to increase your suffering in purgatory. If for the glory of God, God will grant success to your plans; all the Herods in the world could not stand in your way.

**Prayer:** Jesus, if Thou makest me powerless, grant me at least the gift of patience.

**Practise:** Be patient when obstacles present themselves.

ಖಖ⊕ಞಞ

79

## 49 ~ Saturday

"That it might be fulfilled which the Lord spoke by the prophet saying, Out of Egypt have I called my son." ~ St. Matthew (2:15)

**Thought:**  Those events which are often the most contrary to our views and desires are nevertheless planned by Divine Providence in a general way, and also in a particular way as regards yourself. You must not allow yourself to be discouraged by anything that may happen.  The will of God must always be done. The people of God went out of the land of Egypt, where He has been obliged to fly for safety.  Exile is hard to bear, but nothing can injure the worth of Providence. Trial is a necessary preparation for God's work.

**Prayer:**  Jesus, shorten the length of my trial, or increase in me the gift of patience.

**Practise:**  See and recognise the Hand of Providence in all things.

ಬಙ✿ಂಚಜಬಙ✿ಂಚಜಬಙ✿ಂಚ

## 50 ~ Sunday (The Epiphany Week)

"When Jesus therefore was born in Bethlehem of Judah, behold there came wise men from the East to Jerusalem."
~ St. Matthew (2:1)

**Thought:** Admire the almighty power of this little Child, who from His cradle makes known His coming to the shepherds and Magi – to the shepherds by means of His Angel, to the Magi by a star in the East. Admire the docility of these kings. Jesus is born. Behold them at His feet! Let us be little, let us hide ourselves and the Divine Strength will be granted to us. Be docile and quick in following divine inspirations, and you will then become wise of the wisdom of God, powerful of His almighty power.

**Prayer:** Jesus, draw me to Thy crib. Grant that I may recognise Thy voice in the stars, as well as in the Angels – in the natural order, as well as in the supernatural order of things.

**Practise:** Be ever ready to follow good inspirations.

৪০৪০❀ন্মেঙ্গ

## 51 ~ Monday

**"Where is He that is born King of the Jews?"** ~ St. Matthew (2:2)

**Thought:** What boldness and imprudence! How is it that the Magi, alike wise men and kings, have forgotten the suspicious mind of a prince? How comes it that they have not foreseen the danger of compromising either their reputation for wisdom in undertaking such a long journey without learning beforehand something as certain as to the birth of a

King whom they came to adore, or of endangering their life and their kingdoms in coming to render homage to a Prince who is not the son of the reigning King? What a lesson is it not for us! What an example for us who dare not declare ourselves in favour of the royalty of Jesus Christ, fearing lest we should compromise ourselves before the mighty of this world or in the opinion of our friends.

**Prayer:** Jesus, when shall I ever learn for certain that true prudence consists in seeking after *Thee* alone, and in despising the wisdom and power of this world.

**Practise:** Go straight to Jesus.

ಬಙ❀ಅಚ

## 52 ~ Tuesday

**"For we have seen His star in the East, and have come to adore Him."**
**~ St. Matthew (2:2)**

**Thought:** We have also seen, and are come. Let our will respond to our intelligence, our resolution to out thoughts. Such is the characteristic of the Divine working. God said, *Fiat*, "Let there be light, and there was light." Hesitation ruins everything. Of course you should never undertake anything without feeling sure that you are doing the will of God; but once feeling sure, act. The Wise Men *saw* the star and *came* at once. It is only a light, but never mind, follow it. This light will lead you straight to Him who is the Light and

Sun of Justice and Truth. *Et venimus adorare eum.*

**Prayer:** Jesus, give me a quick and ready resolution, so that I may without any hesitation follow the first inspirations of grace.

**Practise:** Be prompt and decisive in following Divine inspirations.

౷౽౿⊕౷౿

## 53 ~ Wednesday

**"And King Herod hearing this, was troubled, and all Jerusalem with him."**
**~ St. Matthew (2:3)**

**Thought:** A Child was the cause of dismay to a whole nation; and an old man will make the powers of this world tremble. Leo makes Attila withdraw, Gregory VII makes Henry IV of Germany grow pale; Pius IX alone and unsupported stays and breaks the most bitter revolutions which cast down kings and cause revolt among people. And you, do you fear the world? Public opinion, the people, the majority –all! All tremble with Herod. *Et omnis Jerosolyma cum illo.*

**Prayer:** Jesus, if Thy weakness is of such strength, what will be Thy real power! If in the early days of Thy human life Thou art so to be feared, what wilt Thou be at the solemn Day of Judgement?

83

**Practise:** Despise the world and all human respect.

೮೩೮ ✿ ೮೩೮

### 54 ~ Thursday

**"And seeing the star, they rejoiced with exceeding great joy." ~ St. Matthew (2:10)**

**Thought:** If you feel no inspiration, follow your reason, or consult your superiors or your director; be guided by faith, and submit with obedience. Do not be discouraged; do not turn back or stand still. Do not stop on the way, save to inquire and obtain necessary information. The day will supersede the night, and the star will shine again to our exceeding great joy.

**Prayer:** Jesus, yesterday all things seemed easy to me, Thy star shone forth; but today all is change, everything seems difficult, the obstacles are insurmountable, for the star has disappeared. Give me grace to use the little light that may be left in me to my greater advantage.

**Practise:** When desolation comes upon you bear in mind that if you are but faithful, consolation will soon follow.

೮೩೮ ✿ ೮೩೮

## 55 ~ Friday

**"And falling down they adored him."**
**~ St. Matthew (2:11)**

**Thought:** The wisdom of the world bends low before a Child; power itself is humbled before impotence; the Wise Men adored the wisdom of God Himself in that little Child; the powerful ones of the earth adored His Power. Let us too believe – by faith we shall know what our reason cannot teach us – we shall see Divine Wisdom in all things, in those events which according to our ideas are most contrary to human prudence; and we shall also recognise the powerful Hand of God even in the reverses with which He visits those who give up everything for love of Him.

**Prayer:** Jesus, give me grace to understand the wisdom of Thy silence, and the strength of Thy feebleness.

**Practice:** Place your trust in God, and in God alone.

ജ്ഞാ ✠ ൙ന

## 56 ~ Saturday

**"They went back another way into their country."** ~ St. Matthew (2:12)

**Thought:** Having once found Jesus, you must

change your route and your conduct. After you have been to Communion, the world is waiting to destroy you, and to destroy Jesus who is in you. You have to battle with Herod and the world, for you must avoid the world, and have no communication with it.

**Prayer:** Jesus, change my thoughts and sentiments. Inspire me with esteem and love for poverty and humility; teach me to hate and contemn the world, its riches and its favours.

**Practise:** Contemn all that the world esteems dear, and esteem all that the word contemns.

൝ഽ൮⊛ര൩ඝ൝ഽ⊛ര൩ඝ൝ഽ⊛ര൩

### 57 ~ Sunday within the Octave of the Epiphany

**"And when He was twelve years old, they were going up into Jerusalem, according to the custom of the feast."** ~ St. Luke (2:42)

**Thought:** Besides the morning and evening prayers that we say each day, there are other prayers which the law of God commands to be offered up for the glory of God, and as thanksgiving for benefits received every day. It is not only advisable, but obligatory, for you to show yourself in the temple of God. If you should refuse to comply with such a command, you would be guilty either of human respect or of contempt of God.

**Prayer:** Jesus, may I never become hypocritical and pretend to be religious when such is not the case; grant likewise that I may never be guilty of human respect, seeking to remain a Christian without appearing as such.

**Practise:** Be as you ought to be, and show yourself as you are.

ಜಜ⊕ಞಚ

## 58 ~ Monday

### "The child Jesus remained in Jerusalem."
### ~ St Luke (2:43)

**Thought:** A child should obey his parents. Jesus never disobeyed His parents; but in those things that concern God, such as prayer, zeal, vocation, penance, inspirations of a supernatural order, these should be allowed to triumph over the sentiments of nature. The Divine Child does not ask permission to remain in Jerusalem, though He would certainly have obtained it; He wishes to give us an example of the holy liberty that a Christian may take in all that concerns the honour of his God.

**Prayer:** Jesus, teach me properly to reconcile the use of true liberty with the respect due to lawful authority.

**Practise.** Follow Divine inspiration without failing in the obedience due to God's representatives here on earth.

සුකා❀ලඥ

## 59 ~ Tuesday

**"They came ... and sought Him among their kinsfolk and acquaintances."**
~ St. Luke (2:44)

**Thought:** Begin by employing natural means; follow the light of reason in the first place. Such is the order of things. God Himself expects that before He enlightens and helps you by His special assistance, you should on your side do your utmost. Generally, however, you will not succeed without having recourse to supernatural means, the principal of which is prayer.

**Prayer:** Jesus, I will seek Thee round about me in those persons with whom Thou wouldst wish to dwell, for I know Thou art generally to be found with or near them. But if I do not find Thee there, where shall I look for Thee?

**Practise:** Do all in your power to find Jesus, remembering that you may always succeed by prayer.

සුකා❀ලඥ

## 60 ~ Wednesday

### "And they found Him in the temple."
### ~ St. Luke (2:46)

**Thought:** You will find Jesus in the temple, in the temple of your heart if you are in a state of grace, or in the Church where the faithful flock to honour Him. Return to the double temple by means of prayer, and there you will meet Jesus when you have in vain looked for Him elsewhere.

**Prayer:** Jesus, grant that through prayer my soul may become a living temple where Thou canst ever dwell.

**Practise:** Ever think of Jesus present in you by His grace.

෨ඥ⊛ඥ౪

## 61 ~ Thursday

### "Son, why hast Thou done this?"
### ~ St. Luke (2:48)

**Thought:** What sweetness and tenderness is there not in this reproach? Is it thus that I complain when separated from Jesus? Alas! No, for often I do not notice the separation, or I am indifferent to it, or I grow irritated and murmur, or am discouraged at the uselessness of my efforts to regain the sensible devotion that I have lost. Thus going from one extreme to another, I grieve Jesus by my indifference, or offend Him by my impatience.

**Prayer**: Jesus, Thou shouldst complain of my conduct; it is not Thou who leavest me, but I who separate myself from Thee by lukewarmness or sin.

**Practice:** In times of desolation be resigned, but not indifferent.

ఴఴఀ❀ఄఄ

## 62 ~ Friday

**"Did you not know that I must be about My Father's business?" ~ St. Luke (2:49)**

**Thought:** God before and above all things! Such is the command, such is the law, and our very reason acknowledges it. Every interest should be sacrificed, every obligation cancelled for the furtherance of this supreme duty. You seek Jesus, you look for consolation and joy of the soul: serve God, pray to Him, and you will thus come face to face with Jesus; you will find the consolations of spiritual joy.

**Prayer:** Jesus, grant that I may only interest myself in what tends to the service and honour of Thy Father.

**Practice:** Have God in sight, and Him only.

ఴఴఀ❀ఄఄ

## 63 ~ Saturday

## "And Jesus advanced in wisdom and age."
### ~ St. Luke (2:52)

**Thought:** It has been said that to conquer is to advance. If then I loiter for one moment on the road to perfection, the world and the flesh get the better of me and I turn back. God, besides, gives His grace in proportion to the efforts that I make. If I bury the talent that God confides to my care, He will take it away altogether; if I increase its value, God will double it. Therefore I shall advance in grace as I advance in wisdom, and I shall advance in wisdom in proportion as I advance in grace. These two things correspond, and form a circle.

**Prayer:** Jesus, I shall never be able to follow Thee unless Thou drawest me towards Thee; and unless I follow Thee Thou wilt cease to draw me towards Thee. I will abandon myself to Thee without reserve.

**Practice:** Make one step forward each day.

ಙಙ✤ಞಞ

## 64 ~ Second Sunday After the Epiphany

**"And there was a marriage in Cana of Galilee, and the mother of Jesus was there."**
**~ St. John (2:1)**

**Thought:** Mary is always where charity calls her. Let us fly all worldly feasts, but let us observe necessary decorum. Contemplate Mary in this family circle; she is not severe or austere, but grave and dignified, full of modesty and charity.

**Prayer:** Jesus teach me how to find the happy medium which accommodates the duties of nature to those of religion, the duty of man to the duty and respect asked of us by God.

**Practise:** You must always study good manners.

ಖಞ✿ಞೞ

## 65 ~Monday

**"And Jesus also was invited, and His disciples, to the marriage." ~ St. John (2:2)**

**Thought:** Jesus deigns to assist at a joyous gathering that He may sanctify it with His presence. Take notice of His bearing, how simple and dignified, and yet how sweet and grave! Listen to His discourse.

Jesus comes with His disciples; and what are they? – Simple fishermen. Behold Him, the Son of kings, accustomed to the company of Mary and Joseph whose very manner and speech were dignified and gentle in the extreme; behold He does not blush to appear in company with these disciples whose manners He has not yet had time to reform. What a lesson of humility!

**Prayer:** Jesus, admit me into Thy company in spite of the vices and defects which make me so intolerable to Thy friends.

**Practise:** Adapt yourself to all classes of men.

శుభం☀రాత్రి

## 66 ~ Tuesday

**"The mother of Jesus saith to him, They have no wine." ~ St. John (2:3)**

**Thought:** Mary is so charitable that she looks to everything that concerns her neighbour, even to temporal concerns. And if this tender mother is so watchful and attentive in small matters, how vigilant and anxious will she not be when it is a question of the interests of a soul, of an eternity!

**Prayer:** Jesus, Mary understands Thy Heart so well. She does not ask Thee for anything but calls Thy attention to what is taking place, knowing full well that discovering a want is enough to excite Thy bounty.

**Practice:** Have confidence in Mary.

୫୬ ❀ ୧୨

## 67 ~ Wednesday

### "Woman, what is it to Me and to thee?"
### ~ St. John (2:4)

**Thought:** What is it? O my Divine Jesus, it is that she is Thy mother, and Thou her Son; a word from her, even the simple statement of the case uncoupled with any wish expressed by her, suffices to hasten on the time of Thy first miracle. Why, then, a reply seemingly so harsh? It is a mystery that I leave to others to unfathom. Perhaps Jesus wished to make us understand that He is ready to anticipate the smallest wish of His mother, even in those things which are beyond the sphere of her maternal rights.

**Prayer:** Jesus, often when Thou art severe to Thine own people, Thou intendest to grant them a great favour.

**Practise:** Ever confide in Jesus.

୫୬ ❀ ୧୨

94

# 68 ~ Thursday

**"Whatsoever He shall say to you, do ye."**
**~ St. John (2:5)**

**Thought:** Mary knew perfectly well that in spite of the apparent severity of His reply, her prayer would be answered. Let us after praying think that God has heard our prayer and let us act accordingly. This is an innocent expedient for doing a sweet violence to the Heart of Jesus.

**Prayer:** Jesus; I wish to do all that Thou hast said. Thou hast said, "Ask, and you will receive." This is enough for me, I shall consider as granted all that I ask of Thee.

**Practice:** Pray with constancy and confidence.

ಐಐಐ✽ಐಐ

# 69 ~ Friday

**"Fill the waterpots with water."**
**~ St. John (2:6)**

**Thought:** And to tell the truth, Jesus is almost compromised by His mother's word. As a dutiful Son He can refuse her nothing, and to obey her He commands mankind and the elements. Let us pray, and even if what we ask were impossible, nothing could resist a prayer, which is all-powerful over the Almighty Himself.

**Prayer:**  Jesus, were I as void of Thy grace as were the jars and water before Thou spakest, the grace and power to pray to Thee would still be left to me, and that would be sufficient to obtain both grace and strength.

**Practice:**  Never cease to pray either in bodily or spiritual affliction.

ಋಷಿ✸ಲೇ


## 70 ~ Saturday

### "And He manifested His glory."
### ~ St. John (2:11)

**Thought:** Two things are necessary for true glory, power and bounty; the former without the latter causes terror, the second without the first inspires contempt.  Unite bounty and power and you will win admiration; add power to bounty and you will win love. All the miracles that Jesus wrought were favours, and all manifested His glory.

**Prayer:**  Jesus, I admire Thee because Thou art great, but I love Thee because Thou art good.

**Practise:** Be neither irresolute nor headstrong, but mild and strong-minded; *suaviter fortiter*.

ಋಷಿ✸ಲೇ

## 71 ~ Third Sunday After the Epiphany

**"And when He was come down from the mountain."** ~ St. Matthew (8:1)

**Thought:** The mountain is heaven, or the bosom of the Eternal Father. The Word, in becoming flesh, came down from heaven out of the Paternal Breast to take upon Himself our nothingness, to raise us up and elevate us even to His Father. Jesus, or the Word made flesh, is God, Who is ever near to us: Let us approach to Him, for He permits us; let us show Him our misery, He will have compassion on us.

**Prayer:** Jesus, Thou hast made the first advance towards me; how can I refuse to reply to such kind attentions, to such touching condescension?

**Practice:** Fidelity to grace.

ಖಖ✿ಐಆ

## 72 ~ Monday

**"Lord, it Thou wilt, Thou canst make me clean."** ~ St. Matthew (8:2)

**Thought:** Thou dost wish it, and I alone can prevent it. I wish to be made clean, I desire it much;

but am I like the leper resolved to do all in my power to obtain it? I should like to regain health, but without having to use the remedy. I am anxious that God should cure me of this evil habit, and yet I am unwilling to make an effort to correct myself.

**Prayer:** Jesus, give me that strength of will and purpose that Thou expectest of me without which Thy grace, however efficacious of itself, can serve me nothing; give me this O God, as Thou only canst give.

**Practice:** Pray earnestly; the grace of prayer is always near at hand.

ಜುಜಂ ✹ ಞೞಲ

## 73 ~ Tuesday

### "See thou tell no man." ~ St. Matthew (8:4)

**Thought:** We should be silent about our good works and our deeds of charity, for silence is the safeguard of merit and success. In boasting of the good you have done, you will there and then have received your reward, and you will have lost it also, for the world refuses to glorify those who seek for glory or look for it as a right. And more than this, if you publish your grand works, the enemies of virtue will league against you in order to hinder your work and to put a stop to your success.

**Prayer:** Jesus, may Thy modesty and prudence serve me as rule and model through life.

**Practice:** Do good, but do it silently.

ಐಖಾ✿ಇಇಚ

## 74 ~ Wednesday

**"Lord, my servant lieth at home sick of the palsy." ~ St. Matthew (8:6)**

**Thought**: When you have lost all strength and feel yourself weak and powerless, speak to Jesus. You have only to expose your wants; He can and will help you. And if He does not help you, it will either be because your prayers have not been fervent enough, or because He intends to confer some still greater benefit to you.

**Prayer:** Jesus, raise me up, waken me. Were it not for Thee my faculties would be numbed, my strength would be paralysed.

**Practice:** Have recourse to Jesus in your weakness.

ಐಖಾ✿ಇಇಚ

## 75 ~ Thursday

**"I will come and heal him." ~ St. Matthew (8:7)**

**Thought:** How kindly and with what readiness

does not Jesus comply with the request of the centurion. Be you likewise ready to assist and help in a spirit of charity when called upon. Do not be numbered among those who, when called upon to oblige a friend, find it quite impossible to comply.

**Prayer:** Jesus, Thou art ready now to assist and help us as when Thou didst walk the earth; come, then, and take pity on my weakness.

**Practice:** Be always willing to oblige others, and God will be willing to help you.

෧෦෧ ⊛ ෨෨

## 76 ~ Friday

### "Lord, I am not worthy." ~ St. Matthew (8:8)

**Thought:** Humble yourself, acknowledge your unworthiness before God and man. Humility never deceives one; or if it does by exaggeration of the contempt of self, it is not on that account exposed to any mistake. One risks very little in estimating one's worth at a lower rate than necessary. One runs the risk of a great danger in overestimating one's worth. God is disarmed by humility; but He remains inflexible towards the proud. Humility disarms mankind, who are unable to support the superiority of true merit, and revolt against a false superiority which pride awards to itself.

**Prayer:** Jesus, I am not worthy that Thou

shouldest approach me in the Holy Eucharist; nevertheless, say but the word to render me less unworthy of Thy Presence.

**Practice:** Never boast of your own acquirements, but think little of yourself.

ಜಬಿ⊛ಚಿಚ

## 77 ~ Saturday

**"Go, and as thou hast believed, so be it done to thee." ~ St. Matthew (8:13)**

**Thought:** Faith is the scale by which the generosity and power of God in our regard is measured out. Not that God does not often, nay, generally, give more than our faith would entitle us to, but in His glory and bounty He is never content to give us less than we expect from His power and His liberality.

**Prayer:** Jesus, I believe, but increase my faith. It is so fragile, the least thing makes it tremble.

**Practice:** Reanimate your faith by the remembrance of what Jesus Christ has promised you.

ಜಬಿ⊛ಚಿಚ

## 78 ~ Fourth Sunday after the Epiphany

### "And behold a great tempest arose."
### ~ St. Matthew (8:24)

**Thought:**  The sea represents the world, and the Church is like unto the boat.  The world at all times rises up against the Church, and indeed against each particular faithful soul.  You have only to wish to do good, and the world with its sea of opinions and miserable passions will turn against you.

**Prayer:**  Jesus, if Thou art in the vessel of my heart, I shall care little about the troubles that surround me.

**Practice**:  Despise the world and all its threats.

ಐಙ ✸ ಛಚಛ

## 79 ~ Monday

### "But He was asleep." ~ St. Matthew (8:24)

**Thought:**  What matter whether Jesus sleeps or not, provided He is there; besides, if He sleeps is it not somewhat through our neglect and forgetfulness?  He sleeps on in the bottom of our boat and leaves us alone to ourselves that we may learn how impotent we are without Him.

**Prayer:**  Jesus, if I were always thinking of

Thee; I should find that Thou art always thinking of me. If I were to speak of to Thee continuously by means of prayer, I should hear Thy word and know that Thou art with me."

**Practice:** Pray always, and never cease to invoke Jesus.

ಉಖಿ✾ಲ೪ಲ

## 80 ~ Tuesday

### "Lord, save us, we perish."
### ~ St. Matthew. (8:25)

**Thought:** It is only at the last moment when our pride is overcome by fear and when we are obliged to recognise our helplessness that we resign ourselves to prayer. God waits but for this acknowledgement of our weakness; He has only to hear our cry of distress to show us at once His power and goodness.

**Prayer:** Jesus, I can only join with Thy apostles and say, Lord, Thou art the master, the controller of the tempests, as well as controller of our lives; however hard we may strive we shall surely perish without Thy help, O Lord! Therefore, O Lord, be merciful and help us.

**Practice:** Have confidence in God, and distrust yourself.

ಉಖಿ✾ಲ೪ಲ

## 81 ~ Wednesday

### "Why are you fearful, O ye of little faith?"
### ~ St. Matthew (8:26)

**Thought:** Be not fearful, but pray. By fear we do an injustice to God. Do you think He lacks either the good-will or the power to save you? But how can I help fearing when death is surrounding me on all sides, you will say. Let those who give themselves up to their passions, who gratify their sensual appetites and feed their imagination, let them tremble; but you, man of faith and reason, man of good-will and prayer, remain calm and resolute within the citadel of your soul.

**Prayer:** Jesus, in the midst of all troubles and tumults I will look up to Thee, confiding trustfully in Thy word and in Thy power.

**Practice:** Place your whole undivided trust in the Divine Goodness and Power.

ಜಜಎ✿ಲ೩೮ಚ

## 82 ~ Thursday

### "He commanded the winds and the sea."
### ~ St. Matthew (8:26)

**Thought:** The winds represent worldly opinion and human passion; the sea represents the world. You must not attempt to govern opinion, or to rule over the world and its passions, they are too unstable. But if you wish for peace here below and are desirous of remaining quiet in the midst of the tempest itself, you will have to be resolute and firm. It is of no use reasoning with those who are incapable of understanding reason; you must command.

**Prayer:** Jesus, speak authoritatively to my heart. One word from Thee will produce a calm over my imagination, my passions, and my feelings.

**Practice:** In times of interior or exterior danger remain clam and resolute.

ಬಞ⊛ಚಿಃ

## 83 ~ Friday

**"But the men wondered." ~ St. Matthew (8:27)**

**Thought:** Mankind as a whole does not understand the power of Our Lord. Its strength of idea limits itself to materialism and it cannot understand how the Church, poor and unendowed without any other safeguard than faith and belief, can dominate and ride triumphantly through the tempests and the storms of nineteen centuries.

**Prayer:** I am astonished at the littleness of my faith in time of storms, for history shows me how Thou hast ever been triumphant through all gales and tempests.

105

**Practice**: Place boundless confidence in the word of Jesus Christ.

ಐಐ❀ಐಐ

## 84 ~ Saturday

### "What manner of man is this?" ~ St. Matthew (8:27)

**Thought:** Who is this man that is mightier than the winds and the sea? And who is He that despises worldly opinions more changeable than the wind, passions more violent and more inconstant than the sea? He is no man, but *God-man*, or a man of God.

**Prayer:** Jesus, I have decided between public opinion and Thy Divine word, between passion and Thy will. I despise all that the world loves, and I detest all that it prefers.

**Practice:** I renounce the world and will belong to Jesus Christ.

ಐಐ❀ಐಐಐ❀ಐಐಐ❀ಐಐ

## 85 ~ Fifth Sunday after the Epiphany

### "The kingdom of heaven is likened to a man that sowed good seed in his field." ~ St. Matthew (8:24)

**Thought:** The field is the world, the master of

the field is God, the good seed is the Divine Word. God sows nothing but good seed. His Word is Truth and Justice. How comes it then that there are men so foolhardy and so impious as to patronise evil and falsehood, expecting as a right for themselves or for others the liberty of proclaiming untruth and blasphemy?

**Prayer:** Jesus, Thy word alone should be echoed in the world and in my heart. Thou alone hast the right of guiding the intelligence and the will.

**Practice:** Listen to God only, who is all Truth and Goodness.

ಬುಃಲ ⊛ ಲಃಲ

## 86 ~ Monday

**"But while men were asleep his enemy came."**
**~ St. Matthew (8:25)**

**Thought:** Whilst those who have won the reputation of being good take their rest in ease and comfort, the scoffer and the sophist sow the seeds of heresy, and the libertine spreads his scandals. What would come to pass if principles of heresy and vice were allowed to spread without condemnation?

**Prayer:** Jesus, place over us superiors who will guard us against false doctrines, and who know how to refute and condemn them.

**Practice:**  Be ever upon the watch, lest you be surprised by the spirit of falsehood.

୫୦୫୦❀ଔଔ

## 87 ~ Tuesday

**"The enemy oversowed cockle among the wheat." ~ St. Matthew (13:25)**

**Thought:**  The enemy is the type of all that is false and evil.  How is it that there are persons who are simple enough to demand as a right the toleration of men whose only aim is to corrupt the heart and soul of others?

**Prayer:** Jesus, inspire me with a holy hatred of these sowers of scandal, whose speech is false and whose work is evil.

**Practise:**  Have nothing to do with the sower of the cockle.

୫୦୫୦❀ଔଔ

## 88 ~ Wednesday

**"Sir, didst thou not sow good seed?"
~ St. Matthew (13:27)**

**Thought:** Jesus never sows anything but the seed of truth.  Truth alone has the right to rule the intelligence of man.  Falsehood has no right to show

108

itself.    One must be very false in judgement or corrupted in heart not to share the indignation of the farmer's servants at the sight of the cockle sown over the field, or to notice without astonishment evil and untruth mixed up and confused with what is good and honest.

**Prayer:**  Jesus, inspire me with a hatred and contempt of vice and falsehood, give me instead a sincere esteem for truth and virtue.

**Practice:**    Be ever on the side of truth and justice.

ಙಙಙ✤ಜಜ

## 89 ~ Thursday

### "The enemy hath done this."
### ~ St. Matthew (8:28)

**Thought:** The enemy watches whilst we slumber; the wicked are generally more active than the good; so also the wide range that is allowed to vice and error will always be fatal to truth and virtue.   The sophist and the corrupter never let an occasion slip by of doing ill, while those who teach the Word of God and who work for God make an effort at first and then fall asleep again, leaving the rest of the undertaking in the hands of Providence – at least this is most often the case.

**Prayer:** Jesus, may I always be on  my guard against the enemy of faith and salvation.

**Practice:**  Watch without ceasing over a good work once begun.

ॐ❀ॐ

## 90 ~ Friday

### "Suffer both to grow until the harvest." ~ St. Matthew (13: 30)

**Thought:**  It was not out of respect for liberty (as certain misguided persons would have it) that Jesus Christ bid the seed and the cockle grow undisturbed until the time of the harvest, but for this sole reason ~ that He feared lest in rooting out the bad seed some part of the good seed might also be rooted out.  You must therefore tolerate vice and error when you are unable to extirpate them without compromising virtue and truth.

**Prayer:**  Jesus, give me prudence together with seal.  Zeal without prudence would mar any good that we might do, while prudence without zeal would cause the overthrow of good by evil.

**Practice:**  Be zealous and prudent.

ॐ❀ॐ

## 91 ~ Saturday

**"Gather up first the cockle ... to burn it."**
**~ St. Matthew (13:30)**

**Thought:** Such is the Divine toleration, ever conformable to reason. Vice and error should only be tolerated when the interests of truth and virtue are at stake, and then they should only be tolerated for the purpose of destroying them altogether. Error and vice should be hated and destroyed.

**Prayer:** Jesus, inspire me with that same hatred of wrong and sin that animated Thee from the first moment of Thy Incarnation. Thy only object in taking upon Thyself our human form was to root out vice and falsehood.

**Practice:** Detest and fight against all that is false or evil.

ಐ౮ ✵ ಐ౮౮ಐ౮ ✵ ಐ౮౮ಐ౮ ✵ ಐ౮

## 92 ~ Sixth Sunday After the Epiphany

**"The kingdom of heaven is like to a grain of mustard seed." ~ St. Matthew (13:31)**

**Thought:** From this little grain the whole plant shoots forth. Likewise the principle of a life of perfection here on earth, and of one of eternal glory and happiness hereafter, may take root and spring from one single inspiration of grace. Do not waste one moment of the time allotted to you, nor say or do anything that may be useless to you hereafter. Each moment of your life that is ill spent imperils your eternal happiness.

**Prayer:** Jesus, grant that I many never forget any of Thy sayings. Each one of them is a grain of mustard seed, which once taking root in the heart can and will grow into an immense tree.

**Practice:** Neglect nothing.

ಬಿಎಂ⊕ಲ್ರಲ್ಗ

## 93 ~ Monday

**"But when it is grown up, it is greater than all herbs." ~ St. Matthew (13:32)**

**Thought:** The least advance made by the soul in the path of grace raises it far above any worldly greatness. A cup of water given to a poor man through love of God has more merit in His eye than the conquest of Asia by Alexander the Great.

**Prayer:** Jesus, give me to understand the true worth and value of Thy grace.

**Practice:** Judge of persons and things, not according to the suggestions of your imagination, but according to faith.

ಬಿಎಂ⊕ಲ್ರಲ್ಗ

## 94 ~ Tuesday

"The grain of mustard seed becometh a tree, so that the birds of the air come and dwell in the branches thereof." ~ St. Matthew (13:32)

**Thought:** Charity is developed by grace, and all who desire it can find shelter therein. This little grain of mustard seed represents the Church and the faithful soul. The Church, at first so small and so imperceptible, is now spreading its branches over the whole world so that all nations can find shelter and protection within it. This is characteristic of the works of God. He begins modestly and with little. He continues almost imperceptibly, and finally He extends His power everywhere – such is the progress and character of grace and sanctity in the faithful soul.

**Prayer:** Jesus, extend in me the knowledge of Thy Divine word, and give me to know Thy grace. Grant that my soul may reach the heights of perfection that Thou hast marked out for her.

**Practice**: Be ever faithful and constant to grace.

৪৩৪০❀৫৫৫৪

## 95 ~ Wednesday

**"The kingdom of heaven is like to leaven."**
**~ St. Matthew (13:33)**

**Thought:** God needs *little* to do much. What is smaller than an atom? And yet out of an atom He made the sun. What is there in a bit of earth? And yet from it He made that living essence of all that is wonderful in the world – viz., man.

**Prayer**: Jesus, never permit me to lose one of Thy sayings, or one single grace.

**Practice:** Make use of the least of God's gifts.

ಌಐ✹ಜಅ

## 96 ~ Thursday

**"Which (leaven) a woman took and hid in three measures of meal." ~ St. Matthew (13:33)**

**Thought:** Obscurity is one of the conditions necessary for progress, just as secrecy is a necessary condition for the success of an enterprise. Hide then from man, disappear from his sight, rest content with the good testimony of your conscience and the glory that you are giving to God alone.

**Prayer:** Jesus, Thou strivest to remain hidden both in Thy Church and in particular souls, and the good Thou dost is none the less real and efficacious.

**Practice:** Say less and do more.

༄༅།༄༅

## 97 ~ Friday

**"And without parables He did not speak to them."** ~ St. Matthew (13:34)

**Thought:** Let us place ourselves on a level with those over whom God wishes us to exercise our influence. We should not hide from them the truth, nor should we seek to lessen its importance; our aim rather should be to put truth before their eyes in such a way that faithful and high-minded souls may clearly understand it, while feeble souls may gradually acquire a knowledge of its beauty, without being dazzled by its splendour.

**Prayer:** Jesus, when shall I understand Thee perfectly, and make others understand Thee too? When I learn to love Thee above everything else, and make others love Thee – then, and then only. The heart helps the understanding; cherished truths are easily understood.

**Practice:** Seek truth everywhere, and in all things.

༄༅།༄༅

**"I will utter things hidden from the foundation of the world." ~ St. Matthew (13:35)**

**Thought:** In heaven only shall we understand this revelation in all its fullness. Nevertheless good and upright souls are admitted here on earth into the Divine secrets. The trials of the just, so mysterious to common people, so misjudged by weak-minded Christians, and so blasphemed by the wicked, need only to be seen with the light of faith to be at once understood. And so it is with a number of other mysteries.

**Prayer:** Jesus, of all hidden mysteries the mystery of the Cross is the most wonderful. Give me to understand how and why it is that the height of infamy may lead to the height of glory – how excess of suffering may produce a fullness of happiness.

**Practice:** Receive with gratitude the lights that faith procures you.

ಐ‍ಐ❀ಎ‍ಐ

ಜಃಏ❀ಚೆಟಜಃಏ❀ಚೆಟಜಃಏ❀ಚೆಟ

## Septuagesima: Liturgical Prelude

ಜಃಏ❀ಚೆಟಜಃಏ❀ಚೆಟಜಃಏ❀ಚೆಟ

### 99 ~ Septuagesima Sunday

"The kingdom of heaven is like to a householder, who went out early in the morning to hire labourers into his vineyard."
~ St. Matthew (20:1)

**Thought:** From the earliest days of my childhood, as soon as ever I came to the use of reason, God through His grace invited me to cultivate His vine – that is, to take care of the natural faculties and supernatural gifts confided to me on the day of my baptism. How have I answered this call?

**Prayer:** Jesus, how much glory should I not have rendered to Thee, and how much merit should I not have acquired, if from the day when reason first dawned had I devoted all my strength, every grace I

117

have received, every minute of my life to Thy service. O irreparable loss!

**Practice:** Do not delay till 'tomorrow', but reply at once to the call of Divine grace.

ಜಜಂ✸ಂಜಆ

### 100 ~ Monday

**"And having agreed with them for a penny a day, he sent them into his vineyard."**
**~ St. Matthew (20:2)**

**Thought:** The day represents life, and payment is heaven, which is the possession of God for all eternity. The vine is the Church. We should spend our whole life in cultivating it, that is, in spreading about the knowledge and love of God, and in sanctifying and saving souls. Time spent otherwise is lost for all eternity.

**Prayer:** Jesus, I make Thee an offering of all my thoughts, desires, words, and deeds.

**Practice:** Work for Jesus, and He shall be your reward.

ಜಜಂ✸ಂಜಆ

## 101 ~ Tuesday

**"And going out about the third hour he saw others standing in the market-place idle."**
**~ St. Matthew (20:3)**

**Thought:**  The market-place represents the world.  There one sees men who move about and come and go, but yet do nothing.  This one bestirs himself to gain a little money, that one is desirous of acquiring fame, a third rushes in pursuit of pleasure which like a phantom escapes his grasp even when he thinks to hold it.

**Prayer:**  Jesus, the day of my life is far advanced, yet I am still in the market-place looking on at what is taking place, listening to what is said, but taking no active part myself.  Come to me, O Jesus, and speak to me!  Another call from Thee will, perhaps, be more efficacious.

**Practice:**  Avoid sloth, and, what is a great deal worse, slothful activity, which on account of its very deceptiveness, should be shunned and feared.

ೞೞ✿ಌಜ

## 102 ~ Wednesday

**"Go you also into my vineyard."**
**~ St. Matthew (20:4)**

119

**Thought:** This vine, as I said before, is the Church. Do not waste your intelligence, your energies, your time, or your fortune in this market-place so truly typical of that world which neither pays not gives back what is lent – of that world ever ungrateful, ever forgetful of favours received; rather consecrate yourself entirely to the service of the Church.

**Prayer:** Jesus, employ me in Thy vineyard. Grant me the only favour that I ask of Thee, viz., to work in Thy service.

**Practice:** Pray for the Church of Jesus Christ. Work in its service, and suffer for it.

ಬಞ⊛ಝಞ

## 103 ~ Thursday

### "Why stand you here all the day idle?"
### ~ St. Matthew (20:6)

**Thought:** Do not allow your whole life to pass in idleness. Do not be always on the point of making a start of doing something, and yet fulfilling nothing. It is not the intention, but the action that is required of you. Take a resolution and keep it – work. All the evils of society owe their origin to the lovers of idleness. Idleness lulls to sleep the minds of the good, and strengthens the minds of the wicked to commit evil with impunity and success.

**Prayer:** Jesus, give me great strength of will.

Tell me what Thou wouldst have me to do, and give me strength and will to accomplish it.

**Practice:** Do your duty, and cease to think of what you ought to be doing yet never do.

ಐ೫ා ✿ ಐ೫

### 104 ~ Friday

### "Is it not lawful for me to do as I will?" ~ St. Matthew (20:15)

**Thought:** God is Master of His gifts. If it pleases Him to give to others the same graces, or even more graces than those which He thinks fit to bestow on me, after having given me what He promised what right have I to complain or murmur? Besides, if I receive less than this or that person, have I not received more than many others? In any case, I have received a great deal more than I deserved since in the beginning I was *nothing*, and therefore deserved nothing.

**Prayer:** Jesus, I admire Thee in others as well as in myself, and thus partaking of other's joy as well as of my own, I shall be doubly happy. My happiness will increase according to the number of those who are happy like myself, and according to their degree of happiness.

**Practice:** Despise jealousy in yourself, as you despise it in others.

## **105 ~ Saturday**

**"So shall the last be first, and the first last."**
**~ St. Matthew (20:16)**

**Thought:** When it is the question of serving God never say, Oh, it is too late! If you have but an hour to live, you can do as much to serve God and deserve heaven as this or that person who has been serving God all his lifetime. Very often it happens that those who from the first accustom themselves to do good end by looking upon it as a duty and perform it habitually like any other actions of their life, and are easily distanced by those souls whose fervour is greater but who have not been so long in the service of God. And again, Jesus bestows His grace according to our good-will; for He is Master of all grace and can bestow more upon the workman who only entered His service at the eleventh hour.

**Prayer:** Jesus, during this day or this hour, which may perhaps be my last, give me grace to atone for all the ill-spent hours, days, and years of my past life.

**Practice:** Do what you have to do, and lose not a moment.

## 106 ~ Sexagesima Sunday

**"And when a very great multitude was gathered together, and hastened out of the cities unto Him, He spoke by a similitude."**
**~ St. Luke (8:4)**

**Thought:** Let us gather round Jesus Christ and He will instruct us; and in our turn let us teach those who come to us to instructed in the word of Christ. Let us be simple towards the simple, and, like our Divine Master, let us choose comparisons that strike the understanding of our hearers. *Sensible* things too often tend to lower and darken the intelligence; we should show how, on the contrary, they are capable of raising and enlightening it.

**Prayer:** Jesus, draw me near to Thee by Thy words; give me courage to leave everything behind to follow Thee and hear Thy word. Permit me to gather round Thee those who forget or ignore Thy Divine word, that they may hear and be overjoyed at Thy preaching.

**Practice:** Be docile to the interior and exterior voice of God.

## "The sower went out to sow his seed."
## ~ St. Luke (8:5)

**Thought:** The sower is Jesus Christ, who, bidding adieu to His hidden life, comes down from Heaven and goes out to sow His seed, i.e., His Divine word. *Semen est verbum Dei* – The seed is the word of God. And Jesus sends out into the world other sowers, viz., the Apostles, Popes, Bishops, Priests, and Doctors. Let us also sow the word of God and spread it by preaching and by discoursing, by means of good books and good conversation, by learned and by simple instruction; *in fine,* let us sow everywhere and at all times. As the sun throws out its light on places which the human eye has never seen, so let us throw out the light of God. He who would only sow the seed that yields for certainty would never sow at all. You must risk ten grains, or even more, to obtain one that will yield you fifty fold.

**Prayer:** Jesus, grant that of all the good seed and light and inspiration which Thou castest into my heart, some as least may fall on good ground and turn to Thy glory.

**Practice:** Profit by the word of God and spread it about.

ಬುಕಾ ✸ ೞಲಣ

## "And some (of the seed) fell by the roadside."
## ~ St. Luke (8:5)

**Thought:** There are some persons whose souls are like the roadside. Everybody passes by it. It is an odd succession of thoughts, desires, impressions and sentiments, which end by hardening the soul just as pedestrians harden the road on which they continually tread. So when the word of God falls on these souls it cannot penetrate but remains upon the surface; and as seed falling by the wayside is soon trodden down by the passers-by or eaten by the birds, so the seed of God, falling upon dissipated and impure minds, is lost or carried away, or trodden under foot by the heavy weight or worldly interest, or by the malice and influence of the devil.

**Prayer:** Jesus, grant that I may carefully preserve all seed that Thou sowest in me. That, like Mary, I may keep all Thy sayings in my heart.

**Practice:** Do not lose one good thought.

శుభం☸దాఅం

## 109 ~ Wednesday

**"And other some fell upon a rock."**
**~ St. Luke (8:6)**

**Thought:** Of what use are good thoughts and intentions unless carried out? Or what will they profit if they are just begun and then left unfinished. You wish to do good, then prepare to encounter much resistance and many obstacles. You will meet with opposition – *cecidit super petram*. Unless you are determined to do good, you will never succeed.

**Prayer:** Jesus, I confide in Thee and in Thee alone. I will deposit in Thy Heart all the good intentions with which Thy grace may inspire me.

**Practice:** Be constant in your good resolution.

ಬಜಂ✺ಞಲ

## 110 ~ Thursday

**"And other some fell among the thorns."**
**~ St. Luke (8:7)**

**Thought:** The thorns represent worldly care. How can the word of God ever be heard in a heart that is always full of passion, worldly thoughts and desires?

If it were heard, it would soon be suffocated in this forest of useless and even guilty thoughts and desires.

**Prayer:** Jesus, may the fire of Thy love burn these thorns which stand so much in my way; grant that I may have but one care, viz., Thee and Thy glory.

**Practice:** Burden yourself with no unnecessary care.

ಜಿಜಿ ⊛ ಜಜ

## 111 ~ Friday

### "And other some fell upon good ground."
### ~ St. Luke (8:8)

**Thought:** The good ground is not hardened like unto the roadside, but it is soft and yielding; the good ground is not arid like the rocky soil, it is humid and fertile; the good ground may be covered with thorns, for thorns, like vice and vicious men, are to be found everywhere, but the husbandman will take care to root them out. Extirpate likewise from your soul all perverse thoughts and affections; water and cultivate it by prayer and frequenting of the sacraments which are channels of grace; open wide your heart to Divine inspiration, and this being done, the seed, i.e., the Divine word and grace, will bring forth an abundant harvest.

**Prayer:** Jesus, surround my heart with a hedge that will preserve me against all false maxims and bad example, water it with Thy Blood, root out from it all vices and dishonest affections and sow in it Thy Divine word.

**Practice:** Be docile, but at the same time be firm and resolute.

ဆာ၈ဎ❀ဎၔဢ

## 112 ~ Saturday

**"But that on the good ground are they who in a good and very good heart, hearing the word, keep it, and bring forth fruit in patience." ~ St. Luke (8:15)**

**Thought:** The seed that falls on good ground takes hold and grows up gradually. A good heart receives the inspirations of grace and holds them firmly; little by little the light appears, the resolution is formed, and the fruit comes forth. One does not, however, become good all in a day. Patience is necessary, not only for the furtherance of holy enterprise inspired by the love of God and neighbour, but also for the perfection of self. This is a lifelong work.

**Prayer:** Jesus, Thou art Thyself the seed, the Word; grant that I may receive Thee and guard Thee; grant that I may sustain myself as Thou hast sustained me.

**Practice:** Do not be discouraged at the sight of your own faults.

బ్ర❀ఆచ్ర బ్ర❀ఆచ్ర బ్ర❀ఆచ్ర

## 113 ~ Quinquagesima Sunday

"Behold we go up to Jerusalem, and all things shall be accomplished which were written by the prophets concerning the Son of man."
~ St. Luke (18:31)

**Thought:** Jesus knows what He will have to suffer in Jerusalem, but nothing stops Him. Let us not turn back at the sight of the Cross. In spite of all that we may have to suffer, let us proceed obediently and submissively, accomplishing our duty. What merit shall we not acquire? What glory do we not render to God by being faithful and constant in little things?

**Prayer:** Jesus, give me invincible courage to do Thy holy will.

**Practice:** Do your duty, and leave the rest to God. He will arrange all things.

బ్ర❀ఆచ్ర

## 114 ~ Monday

**"They will put Him to death, and the third day He shall rise again." ~ St. Luke (18: 33)**

**Thought:** It is to no purpose that you turn your back upon the Cross. The world has its cross as well as religion. The cross of the world is but a faint shadow of that of hell. What are the sufferings and humiliations of the libertine when compared to those of the Christian? What are they in comparison to eternal ignominy and everlasting punishment?

**Prayer:** Jesus, I wish to die upon the cross with Thee, that with Thee I may also rise again. Thy Cross raises man above the earth and above himself, is borne but for a short while and brings after it eternal glory and eternal happiness.

**Practice:** Carry the cross which each day brings with it.

ಬಿಷ್ಟ ✠ ಲಿ೦ಚ

## 115 ~ Tuesday

**"And they (the Apostles) understood nothing of these things." ~ St. Luke (18:34)**

**Thought:** The language of the Cross is difficult to understand. Humiliation and suffering are things distasteful and repugnant to nature. The soul refuses humiliation and the body rejects suffering. We do not understand that glory is bought by disgrace, that happiness is purchased by grief; and yet does not real glory principally consist in despising the contempt and the esteem of the world. To experience real happiness, should we not feel strength and liberty enough to suffer anything rather than lose the sole supreme good, which is God Himself?

**Prayer:** Jesus, give me to understand the happiness and greatness that is to be found in despising the contempt of the world, and the sorrows and griefs that are in it. Such contempt is superhuman. It is angelic; it is Divine.

**Practice:** Contempt of humiliation and suffering.[2]

2 Fr. Marin seems to be saying here, judging from his previous meditation (#114) the world makes its own followers suffer too in order to give them its false, failing glory that will eventually end. We should have contempt for what the world demands us to suffer for its false promises, which is different from the sufferings we endure from the world for following Christ. Whatever we endure for Christ will bring an everlasting reward, and in this case we should have contempt towards the fear that discourages us to take on those types of sufferings and humiliations.

ಬಾ❀ಡಡಙಬಾ❀ಡಡಙಬಾ❀ಡಡ

## Lenten Tide

ಬಾ❀ಡಡಙಬಾ❀ಡಡಙಬಾ❀ಡಡ

### <u>116 ~ Ash Wednesday</u>

**"But he cried out much more."
~ St. Luke (18:39)**

**<u>Thought:</u>** You must persevere in prayer, and ask and pray until you receive. Jesus wills to be beseeched that He may prove the sincerity of your desire and the constancy of your will. When man stands in the way of your good works do not lose courage; continue to pray, but address your prayers to God, not to man. Man is not to be relied upon.

**Prayer:** Jesus, I am blind and cannot see my way. I am unable to walk. I can do nothing for Thee. Restore my sight, O Jesus; raise me up, that I may walk in Thy paths and walk in Thy service.

**Prayer:** Pray until your prayer is granted.

ಬಐ❀ಲಚ

## 117 ~ Thursday After Ash Wednesday

**"And Jesus standing, commanded him to be brought unto Him." ~ St. Luke (18:40)**

**Thought:** How powerful is prayer! By a single word Joshua stayed the sun in its course, and by one prayer the poor blind man stopped the Creator of this sun. If you are unable to go to Jesus, pray to Him incessantly and Jesus will wait for you, or will send a guide to conduct you to Him.

**Prayer:** Jesus, call me to Thee; if my fellow-creatures refuse to receive me, Thou at least, O God, wilt receive me.

**Practice:** Confidence and constancy in prayer.

ಬಐ❀ಲಚ

## 118 ~ Friday After Ash Wednesday

## "Lord, that I may see." ~ St. Luke (18:41)

**Thought:** Why have I not the same zeal and constancy in seeking spiritual light as this blind man had in trying to procure bodily sight? If Jesus so easily grants a demand for corporal blessings, how much more easily will He not hear our prayers when we beg spiritual blessings? But alas! With regard to spiritual things I do not even perceive that I am blind.

**Prayer:** Jesus, grant that I may see all that is wanting in me towards truly serving and pleasing Thee, that I may see the vanity of passing things and the truth of those which are lasting.

**Practice:** Consult Jesus incessantly by means of prayer.

ಬಿಙ಼❀ೞೞ

## 119 ~ Saturday After Ash Wednesday

## "Receive thy sight; thy faith hath made thee whole." ~ St. Luke (18: 42)

**Thought:** When reason is blinded by passion, it can hardly distinguish good from evil. Faith restores to us our intelligence and the use of reason. Faith triumphs over every obstacle. God takes pleasure in granting the requests of those who persist in their belief and confide in Him.

**Prayer:** Jesus, I too would imitate the example of the blind man, who when cured immediately followed Thee. I desire to see, that I may follow Thee and bring my soul to Thee. Cured myself, I would gladly teach others to follow Thee.

**Practice:** Follow Jesus by faith.

ಖಖಿ❀ಞಚಿ

## 120 ~ First Sunday in Lent

**"Then Jesus was led by the Spirit into the desert, to be tempted by the devil."**

**~ St. Matthew (4:1)**

**Thought:** The Holy Ghost leads us into the desert, away from the world and its glory. The spirit of the world teaches us to show ourselves and to seek for admiration; but even in the desert we are liable to be tempted by the devil. We can never meet with repose and security in this world.

**Prayer:** Jesus, sustain me, and do not permit me to be tempted above my feeble strength.

**Practice:** Fly from the world and seek solitude.

ಖಖಿ❀ಞಚಿ

## 121 ~ Monday

**"And when He had fasted forty days and forty nights, afterwards He was hungry."**
**~ St. Matthew (4:2)**

**Thought:** You should prepare for the combat by fasting. Begin by conquering yourself. When the soul has once triumphed over the senses and the flesh, you will then be prepared to attack the enemy without. Feebleness of body very often gives strength to the soul.

**Prayer:** Jesus, give me to understand the efficacy of mortification, of which Thou hast given me the example by Thy forty-day's fast; grant that I may practise this mortification.

**Practice:** Mortify yourself continually.

ಬುಕಾ☸ಞೞ

## 122 ~ Tuesday

**"Not in bread alone shall man live, but in every word that proceedeth from the mouth of God." ~ St. Matthew (4:4)**

**Thought:** As bread is the nourishment of the body, so is the Word of God the nourishment of the soul. But the bread becomes part of our flesh and blood; the Word of God, on the contrary, transforms the soul. If we have faith in the Divine Word, our thoughts become divine. How happy and glorious our life would be if we could only think as God thinks and have no other will than God's will!

**Prayer:** Jesus, Thou art the Divine Word, the Word made flesh, the Word made visible. To whom then shall we go. Thou, and Thou alone, hast the word of eternal life.

**Practice:** Live by faith, and by the word of Jesus Christ.

ಬುಕ್ಕ❀ಀಲೞ

## <u>123 ~ Wednesday</u>

### "Thou shalt not tempt the Lord thy God."
### ~ St. Matthew (9:7)

**Thought:** We need not do anything wonderful or extraordinary; let us follow the beaten track and do as others do, only doing better. Let us distinguish ourselves by our retirement and love of solitude. True beauty is the rare assemblage of all ordinary perfection in one person. So it is with sanctity, which is the greatest beauty one can have. A saint only does what others do, but he does that well and for God alone.

**Prayer:** Jesus, give me that pure and upright simplicity which never swerves from right to left, which is never raised but which is never lowered, which, *in fine*, draws us to Thee and to Thee alone.

**Practice**: Perform your ordinary actions well.

ಐಐ❀ಐಐ

## 124 ~ Thursday

**"All these will I give Thee, if falling down Thou wilt adore me." ~ St. Matthew (4:9)**

**Thought:** We must fall down to obtain worldly power. The world gives its favours, honour, and applause to those only who cringe and beg and flatter. Who is more crafty, servile, and stooping than the ambitious man? And what does one gain by such baseness? The world promises what it has not power to give. Honour and power are not at her command. God and man are the only dispensers of these gifts. Men have nothing but contempt for the ambitious, and God seems to delight in frustrating the hopes of this wretched class of people.

**Prayer:** Jesus, give me strength to resist the promises of the world and snares of the devil.

**Practice:** Despise servility and ambition.

ಐಐ❀ಐಐ

## 125 ~ Friday

**"Begone, Satan, for it is written, The Lord thy God thou shalt adore, and Him only shalt thou serve." ~ St. Matthew (4:10)**

**Thought:** Be hard and severe towards Satan.

Consider as coming from him all thoughts, actions or sayings of the world which are contrary to God.

**Prayer:**  Jesus, Thou art my Saviour, my God! Thou art my Master, I will obey only Thee and those who take Thy place here on earth.  I will serve none other than Thee, for Thou only canst complete in me Thy work and procure my salvation.

**Practise:** Seek God and God alone.

ಜುಙಾ❀ಞಲ೮ಽ

## 126 ~ Saturday

**"Then the devil left Him, and behold angels came and ministered to Him."**
**~ St. Matthew (4:11)**

**Thought:** After the fight comes glory, so after the departure of the devil the good Angel comes.  Such is life here on earth, a continual fluctuation from good to evil thoughts, a perpetual combat between the good and bad spirits.  Stand firm in the hour of trial and the hour of comfort will soon draw near.

**Prayer:**  Jesus, sustain my courage during this fight with hope of victory.

**Practice:**  Be confident in time of trial.

## 127 ~ Second Sunday in Lent

**"Jesus taketh unto Him Peter and James and John." ~ St. Matthew (17:1)**

**Thought:** Word and example are given to all, but special manifestations are reserved for the chosen few. Do not aim at celebrity, nor wish to be known by everybody. Jesus shows Himself in secret, and in solitude on a high mountain. You must walk out of the common paths if you would aspire to elevation of thought and desire, which are rays of the glory of Jesus.

**Prayer:** Jesus, raise my thoughts and desires above worldly care and interest; grant that I may dwell in heaven, by the elevation of my heart and my intelligence.

**Practice:** Love of solitude.

## 128 ~ Monday

**"And He was transfigured before them." ~ St. Matthew (17:2)**

**Thought:** As light precedes darkness, so consolation is offered to us before our trials. Jesus is transfigured before the three apostles whom He has chosen to witness His sufferings and His agony. In this moment of glory He speaks of the ignominious death that awaits Him and of the suffering of His Passion; in the midst of His sufferings and His most bitter Passion He speaks of the glory that awaits Him, when, clothed in power and majesty He will descend upon a cloud to judge the judges of this world.

**Prayer:** Jesus, when Thou raisest me by consolation let me call to mind my past destitution; let me think of what I may have to suffer in future time; but when Thou thinkest fit to humble me by affliction, discover to me Thy glory and power.

**Practice:** Be hopeful in time of trial, and fearful in time of success.

৪৩৪৩ ❀ ৫৩৫৪

### 129 ~ Tuesday

**"And behold, there appeared to them Moses and Elias talking with Him."**
**~ St. Matthew (17:3)**

**Thought:** Moses represents the law, Elias the prophets. All bears reference to Jesus Christ. The law is the road which leads to Him, and prophecy is the voice that tells of Him. Our actions are conformed to His will according to the law, and through the prophets our word is likened to His thought. If we keep the law we shall be just through His justice; if we believe the prophecies and the inspired writings we shall be wise with His wisdom.

**Prayer:** Jesus, speak to me in the depths of my heart; recall Thy law and Thy faith continually to my mind; give me grace to believe what Thou commandest and to practise what I believe.

**Practice:** Regularity and faithfulness.

ಜ಼ಾ❀ಌಃ

## 130 ~ Wednesday

### "Lord, it is good for us to be here."
### ~ St. Matthew (17:4)

**Thought:** It seems good for us to be upon Mount Thabor; but it seems less good to be upon Calvary. It is easy to stay with Jesus when all is smooth and tranquil, but it is less easy to persevere in times of affliction and sadness. Let us prove our love for Jesus Christ by standing firm in time of trial. Herein true love is proved.

**Prayer:** Jesus, one ray of Thy glory is enough to make me forget the whole world. Give me from time to time a ray of this light to sustain me on the cross. Calvary would be insurmountable if it were not situated between Thabor and Mount Olivet.

**Practice:** From Thabor look towards Calvary, from Calvary look towards Thabor.

ಜ಼ಾ❀ಌಃ

## 131 ~ Thursday

**"This is my beloved Son, in whom I am well pleased."** ~ St. Matthew (17:5)

**Thought:** Jesus sometimes speaks to me Himself; at other times He speaks by His messengers, or by the inspirations of Divine grace; or again, by the mouth of the preacher; sometimes, too, by events demonstrative of His Divine will in my regard; and finally, by means of those whom He has placed over me to direct my conduct. In whatever way He speaks to me He is always the same; He is ever the beloved Son of God the Father. Let us listen to His word, believe its teaching and act according to its precepts.

**Prayer:** Jesus, Thou shalt be my light and my guide, for Thou only hast the word of eternal life.

**Practice:** Be docile to the call of Jesus.

ಋಐಐ❀ಞಲ

## 132 ~ Friday

**"Arise, and fear not."** ~ St. Matthew (17:7)

**Thought:** We should prepare ourselves for action by contemplation; consolation disposes us for the combat. You cannot always be on Mount Thabor. Arise, go forth courageously and combat the world. Jesus sends you, you need not fear.

**Prayer:** Jesus, I will go, but on one condition, that Thou also enter the field of battle with me.

**Practice:** Confide in God alone.

ಬಿಎಂ✵ಌಚಿ

## 133 ~ Saturday

**"Tell the vision to no man, till the Son of man be risen from the dead."**
**~ St. Matthew (17:9)**

**Thought:** We should not make known what favours we receive, for the world cannot understand them. On the contrary, we should hide ourselves and all our thoughts, actions, and desires. All we have in view is the glory and service of God; our own glory will not suffer by our silence, for it will all be acknowledged on that final and decisive Day of Judgement.

**Prayer:** Jesus, I wish to be ignored as Thou wast ignored; is not Thy esteem and Thy approval enough for me?

**Practice:** Desire to be thought little of.

ಬಿಎಂ✵ಌಚಿ

ಐಐ ✵ ಐ೦ಐಐ ✵ ಐ೦ಐಐ ✵ ಐ೦

## 134 ~ Third Sunday in Lent

**"And He was casting out a devil, and the same was dumb." ~ St. Luke (11:14)**

**Thought:** This dumb devil is typical of human respect, for he is master and tyrant when our courage fails us, when we feel ashamed to declare ourselves Christians, when we are too cowardly to defend Christ and His Church, when, *in fine*, we are ashamed to denounce the blasphemy of the impious or the baseness of the libertine. It is this same devil who frightens the penitent from (coming to) the confessional and makes him feel ashamed of his sins. You are ashamed to confess your sins; then Satan will remain master of your heart and will lead you to perdition.

**Prayer:** Jesus, cast out from my heart all cowardly fear and all false shame; let me never more be guilty of such injustice to Thy greatness and Thy goodness.

**Practice:** Profess your faith openly, confess your faults humbly.

ಐಐ ✵ ಐ೦

**"The dumb spoke, and the multitudes were in admiration at it."** ~ St. Luke (21:14)

**Thought:** Such is the effect of human respect upon the mind, that once having fallen to its power we feel unable to regain our liberty. How can we ever dare to show ourselves and speak our mind freely? The world will be amazed, what will it say of us? We have but to speak, to openly declare our sentiments, and this same world, whose very look was enough to make us tremble and turn pale – this very world, I say, will be entirely disconcerted, and will admire where we expected it to find fault.

**Prayer:** Jesus, never let it be said that I am ashamed of Thee.

**Practice:** Never be guilty of human respect.

ಜಖ೮⊕ೕೕೞೞ

## 136 ~ Tuesday

**"He casteth out devils by Beelzebub, the prince of devils."** ~ St. Luke (11:15)

**Thought:** No matter what you do, the world will have its say. You perform good works – the world puts them down as performed out of pride; you are silent, spend much time in solitude – the world will say that you are disdainful or think yourself above society. Do not mind, Jesus was accused of being in league with the prince of devils. The disciple is not greater than his Master.

**Prayer:** Jesus, grant that I may despise the contempt shown me by the world, which is so foolish in its judgements.

**Practice:** Despise public opinion.

಩ಡಿ✿ಞಲ

## 137 ~ Wednesday

**"Every kingdom divided against itself shall be brought to desolation."**
**~ St. Luke (11:17)**

**Thought:** The wicked hate the Church, and in this alone they are of one mind. See how they fight one against the other! They despise one another and not without good reason, for they know the baseness of each other's minds. They hate one another because each is covetous of his neighbour's goods. They are impediments to each other's progress, and are therefore enemies. And how they fight! You have but to enter the lists, and victory is certain.

**Prayer:** Jesus, Thou alone art able to establish and maintain unity among men. Thou alone art Truth. Thou alone art Charity.

**Practice:**  Be united to Christ by faith and charity.

ಐಐ ✤ ಐಐ

## 138 ~ Thursday

**"When a strong man armed keepeth his court, those things are in peace which he possesseth."** ~ St. Luke (11:21)

**Thought:**  This strong-armed man is the devil, and the court he keepeth is the soul when in a state of mortal sin.  Satan reigns in triumph over those who have rendered him allegiance by sin, until by His grace Jesus drives out the usurper from this kingdom.

**Prayer:**  Jesus, it will avail me little if after driving the devil from my heart Thou dost not close the entry to it and keep watch, for Satan is roving about like a hungry lion seeking for admittance.

**Practice:**  Be ever on the watch, for Jesus, though He is willing to reign over all free hearts, will not protect your heart unless you watch also.

ಐಐ ✤ ಐಐ

## 139 ~ Friday

**"He that is not with me is against Me; and he that gathereth not with Me scattereth."**
**~ St. Luke (11:23)**

**Thought:** Avaunt, you who would serve two masters, who would fight for Christ *and* Belial! Avaunt, you smooth-faced ever-smiling worldlings, who look with pleasure on Mother Church *and* smile benignantly at the prospect of a revolution! You are afraid to declare yourself for Christ then you declare against Him. You are ashamed to decry the impious and the wicked, then by this very shame you become a friend and confederate of the impious and wicked. You cannot call yourself a follower, friend, or brother, member of the Body of Jesus Christ, for the hand protects the head and the arm defends the heart.

**Prayer:** Jesus, give me to understand that all my thoughts, words and actions that are not offered up to Thee by grace and by intention are lost for all eternity.

**Practice:** Declare yourself one of Christ's followers.

෩෨෯෴

## 140 ~ Saturday

"And the last state of that man becomes worse than the first." ~ St. Luke (11:26)

**Thought:** A bad Christian is worse than a bad pagan, a bad Catholic is worse than a bad Protestant, and a bad priest is worse than anyone, except perhaps an apostate monk such as Martin Luther; and he who abuses the great grace of conversion falls much deeper into sin than before, because he falls from a higher eminence.

**Prayer:** Jesus, strengthen me in my weakness, bear me up with Thy grace; Thou alone canst hold Thy own in me against Satan.

**Practice:** Make good use of grace.

೫೫ ✿ ೧೮೫೫ ✿ ೧೮೫೫ ✿ ೧೮

## 141 ~ Fourth Sunday in Lent

"And a great multitude followed Him."
~ St. John (6:2)

**Thought:** If you wish the multitude to follow you, work wonders – that is, perform wondrous acts of kindness, for such is the secret of the success of our Lord and the Church. People are attracted by prodigies of goodness and virtue, such as relieving the necessitous and the poor; but directly Jesus attempted to raise the people's minds from the thought of temporal blessings to that of spiritual by promising them Bread from Heaven in place of that which was perishable, they at once cried out, "Durus est hic sermo." This language is hard, and who can listen to it?

**Prayer:** Jesus, may I follow Thee, not for Thy benefits and Thy goodness, but for Thyself alone. Thou art my only love.

**Practice:** Be united to Jesus only.

ಜಜ಼ ❀ ಞಜ಼

## 142 ~ Monday

### "Jesus therefore went up into a mountain."
### ~ St. John (6:3)

**Thought:** Jesus does not seek the crowd; He contents Himself with doing good, preaching truth and conferring His favours on those who approach Him. In this way He gains a reputation for wisdom and bounty, and is soon followed by an admiring crowd. He withdraws Himself as much as possible; He raises Himself above the affairs and men of this world.

**Prayer:** Jesus, Thou shalt be the mountain where I will take refuge against the multitude of thoughts, passions, and desires, which are ever surrounding me and which distract my attention from Thee and stop me in my search after Thee, my only good.

**Practice:** Make a sanctuary for yourself in the Heart of Jesus, and unite your prayers with His.

ಐಐ✿ೞೞ

## 143 ~ Tuesday

**"Whence shall we buy bread, that these may eat?"** ~ St. John (6:5)

**Thought:** When you feel it impossible to proceed do not lose courage, continue to hope. Acknowledge your helplessness, and God will come to your assistance. If you confide in your own strength, you are sure to fail. And why should we have such confidence in self? Have we not scores of times experienced how powerless are our efforts? Why should we so distrust Our Lord, when He invites us to confide in Him? Has He not promised us His help? And have we not already had proofs of His power and kindness?

**Prayer:** Jesus, I acknowledge my weakness. Without Thee I can find no means of saving souls.

**Practice:** Despise yourself, but trust in God.

ಐಐ✿ೞೞ

## 144 ~ Wednesday

### "Make the men sit down." ~ St. John (6:10)

**Thought:** If you only do your best, God will do the rest. Begin your work and God will consummate it. Be prudent, but do not mistrust. Never undertake on your own responsibility anything that is impossible; but if God commands you to do what may seem impossible, even if it be to feed five thousand persons with five loaves, be obedient to His word and do as you are bid. "Make the men to sit down." It is in your power to do this much.

**Prayer:** Jesus, I will be docile and obedient, and will trust to Thee for success.

**Practice:** Do well all that you have to do.

ಖುಞ✿ಞಲ

## 145 ~ Thursday

### "And Jesus took the loaves." ~ St. John (6:11)

**Thought:** Whatever you possess, you should make good use of it. You have a little; turn that little to good account. You possess but little; give little, but at least give something. You have perhaps received but one talent; do not bury it in the ground. Make use of the intellect, knowledge, will, power, health, wealth, and grace that are given you. The little you have, if taken care of, will increase through the bounty of the Almighty.

**Prayer:** Jesus, take Thou possession of all I have.

**Practice:** Give yourself up entirely to Jesus Christ.

ಜ್ಞಾಡ❀ಡಾಜ

## 146 ~ Friday

## "Gather up the fragments that remain."
## ~ St. John (6:12)

**Thought:** You should not allow any portion of God's gifts to be lost. Do not lose one moment of that time allotted to you by God; time so precious, that God only gives it to us in small portions, so afraid is He lest we should wantonly squander it. Lose not a single thought, word, or action. If God keeps count of the pieces of bread that were over, how much more will He demand an account of each idle word.

**Prayer:** Jesus, give me to understand that all is lost which cannot be referred to Thee or to Thy Father's glory; yes, lost for all eternity.

**Practice:** Never waste your time.

ಜ್ಞಾಡ❀ಡಾಜ

**"Jesus fled again into the mountain Himself alone." ~ St. John (6:15)**

**Thought:** The people wish to make Jesus King, and Jesus flies to the mountains. So when the world would wish to bestow praises upon you, you should take refuge in flight with the good and pure intention of seeking only God, and God's service and His glory in searching after souls and striving for their salvation, not in seeking for their esteem and affection. Raise yourself above the power of this world by raising your heart in prayer. This will render you great and powerful before God, and in God's name.

**Prayer:** Jesus, why should I seek for worldly power and glory? That I may glorify Thee and save souls? No; for Thou, O Jesus, didst refuse worldly glory and worldly power and we should follow Thy example.

**Practice:** Seek not for reputation or worldly honour.

ಜುಜು✠ಚುಜು

## Passion Tide

ಖಞ ✠ ಲಚಚಖಞ ✠ ಲಚಚಖಞ ✠ ಲಚಚ

## 148 ~ Passion Sunday

**"But if I say the truth, why do you not believe Me?" ~ St. John (8:46)**

**Thought:** You can reproach Me with no sin, and therefore with no lie. I only tell you the truth, why then do you not believe Me? If Jesus could have spoken thus to the Jews who did not believe in His Divinity, what could He not say to the Christians who know that He is God and yet refuse to believe His word: or, if they believe, refuse to conform their conduct to their belief?

**Prayer:** Jesus, I believe; but I do not act upon my belief. I know that my life should be one of poverty, humility, and docility. Grant that for the future my conduct in life may coincide with my profession of faith and doctrine.

**Practice:** Let your faith be entire, sincere, and practical.

ഇൽ⊕ൽ


### 149 ~ Monday

**"He that is of God, heareth the word of God." ~ St. John (8:47)**

**Thought:** Fidelity to grace implies preventing grace.[3] God gives sufficient grace to all men; but woe to him who resists the first impulse! He deserves the withdrawal of all those graces that are to follow, and he exposes himself to the danger of becoming insensible to the very graces that God in His bounty deigns to send him.

**Prayer:** Jesus, without Thy aid I cannot make use of grace, but, unhappily, have power to resist it. Grant that I may never misuse this liberty, this power which Thou hast given me to serve Thee with and to save my soul, but not to offend Thee and to cause my own damnation.

**Practice:** Be docile to grace.

ഇൽ⊕ൽ

---

3    Meaning, the call to be be faithful to grace also implies we may be unfaithful to this call and fail to act upon the graces received, thereby 'preventing' grace.

157

## 150 ~ Tuesday

### "But I seek not My own glory."
### ~ St. John (8:50)

**Thought:**  You must forget awhile all self-interest and all self-glory and think only of God's interest and glory; and if you do, you will find that sooner or later in spite of every obstacle you will succeed in your undertakings; and to God, who never allows anyone to outdo Him in generosity will surely not be forgetful of your interest.  The world itself, so severe towards those who push themselves forward and demand notice, will hasten to acknowledge those who sink all thought of self in their desire of doing good to others.

**Prayer:**  Jesus, I only seek for Thy glory.  My sole aim is that Thou shouldst be known and loved and served.  Grant that all my thoughts, words, and actions may ever take their origin from this one desire.

**Practice:**  Have God always in view.

ಖಞ✾ಞಛ

## 151 ~ Wednesday

### "If any man keep My word, he shall not see death for ever." ~ St. John (8:51)

**Thought:**  Jesus is the Life, and why?  Because

He is the Word and the Truth. Truth is life, inasmuch as it is the intellectual life – that is, the life of the soul. Keep the word of Jesus. Think as Jesus thought and speak as Jesus spoke: act in accordance with His word, and you shall live for ever. The death of the soul separates us from God. Keep the word of God by faith and charity. Faith makes your thought and intelligence conformable to the Divine word, and charity makes your action and your will likewise conformable to it, so that you will live eternally.

**Prayer:** Jesus, be to me the Life; never let me forget Thy word; may I follow its precepts in everything.

**Practice:** Keep before you some saying of Jesus Christ.

ಬಂಚ ✿ ಚಲಚ

### 152 ~ Thursday

### "Whom does Thou make Thyself?"
### ~ St. John (8:53)

**Thought:** Do not be afraid to show yourself as you are. Incline less to the multitude and to public opinion, and incline more to Holy Church. Our Mother Church has condemned certain doctrines which public opinion still upholds. You are wiser than the infallible Doctor; and you think it imprudent to condemn what the Pope condemns? "Who does thou make thyself?" *Quem te ipsum facis?"* Are you Christian? Are you Catholic?

159

**Prayer:**   Jesus, grant that I may never feel ashamed to declare myself Thy follower, an obedient and faithful disciple of Thy Vicar here on earth.

**Practice:**   Proclaim the doctrine of the Church, and loudly protest against error.

ಙಞ❀ಜಞ

### 153 ~ Friday

## "Before Abraham was made I Am."
## ~ St. John (8:58)

**Thought:**   Let us serve Him who is before Abraham.   Here below man is born and dies, man passes away:  God alone has no beginning and no end, He passes not away.  Jesus does not say "I was," but "I Am".  Jesus is not of the past, nor of the future.  All our thoughts, words and actions – all that we do for Jesus partake in some degree of His Eternity.  We perform a passing act of goodness, and are rewarded for ever and ever.  The grace with which it was performed stamps it with God's seal and it bears fruit for ever.

**Prayer:**   Jesus, Thou alone dost live for ever – man is ever passing away in death.  I will belong to Thee, and Thee only.

**Practice:**   Unite all your intentions to those of Jesus Christ.

ಙಞ❀ಜಞ

"They took up stones therefore to cast at Him; but Jesus hid Himself, and went out of the temple." ~ St. John (8:59)

**Thought:** This is the only answer that passion makes to reason, heresy to faith – viz., violence. Ye sophists, you are so certain of the triumph of your own ideas? If thus it be, allow the Church the liberty of teaching and instructing. What fear you? Besides, violence is powerless. The Church escapes your fury and in spite of all prevention she pursues her object in secret when she cannot pursue it in public.

**Prayer:** Jesus, grant that I may seek safety from violence of enemies of faith and goodness in retreat.

**Practice:** Unite prudence to firmness in all your actions.

৪০৪০ ✪ ৻৵৻৪০৪০ ✪ ৻৵৻৪০৪০ ✪ ৻৵৻

## 155 ~ Palm Sunday

"And when they drew nigh to Jerusalem, and were come to Bethphage, unto Mount Olivet." ~ St. Matthew (21:1)

**Thought:** What a contrast on this Mount Olivet today! This, a day of triumph for Our Lord, will soon be followed by His Sacred Passion, which begins with His agony and the disturbance in the garden and which is finally consummated by His death – and after death there is His triumph of the Ascension. Such is our life too. We taste the sweetness of success today, tomorrow we shall drink the bitter cup of disappointment. Yesterday we were praised and spoken well of, today we are blamed and reviled. We are filled with consolation now, but and in a short while we shall taste desolation. And it is by these successions of light and darkness that we obtain eternal light, and finally enjoy the certain triumph of the Ascension.

**Prayer:** Jesus, sustain and console me in times of spiritual darkness; whether Thou art hidden or visible it matters not, so long as Thou art present unto me.

**Practice:** Be tranquil and even-minded in the midst of present troubles and difficulties.

ಜ್ಞಾನ⊕ಅಲ

## 156 ~ Monday

**"You shall find an ass tied, and a colt with her; loose *them* and bring *them* to Me."** ~ St. Matthew (21:2)

**Thought:** The ass here represents the ancient people of God tied by the law of God. (The Jews). The colt, which is free and not yet broken in, is typical of the Gentiles. It is the duty of the apostles to bring both to Jesus. The ass reminds us of those habitual vices which chain us fast within their domain. The colt tells us of those sudden outbursts which carry us from the path of good. Again, the ass represents those persons of the world who perform everything by routine and give themselves up to idleness and are neglectful of their duty; while the colt is emblematical of those persons who are ruled by a spirit of pride, anger, or impatience. If you are desirous that Jesus should enter into your heart, submit yourself wholly to His guidance, make Him an offering of your habits and your passions.

**Prayer:** Jesus, here am I before Thee with all my inclinations and all my imperfections, dispose of me according to Thy pleasure.

**Practice:** Fight against your faults, and more especially against those to which you are most subject.

ಙಙ❀ಚಚ

## 157 ~ Tuesday

### "Say ye that the Lord hath need of them."
### ~ St. Matthew (21:3)

**Thought:** Everything gives way before those words, "The Lord hath need." When God wills anything it must be done, in spite of the opposition of the world; no matter how reasonable this opposition may appear it will give way to the will of God. When therefore Our Lord commands, go you and obey His summons. How unprecedented is this command, Go loosen and bring with you an animal, the property of another, and do this in the presence of the owner, without even asking his permission! The Master of masters has spoken; obey, and all will happen as He desires, as He has foretold.

**Prayer:** Jesus, if Thou didst command me to do that which seems impossible, I would obey. *Da quod jubes, et jube quod vis* – I will do what Thou commandest, but command what Thou pleasest.

**Practice:** Obey at once, and without reasoning.

ಜಜಿ⊕ಡಗ

### 158 ~ Wednesday

**"Tell ye the daughter of Sion: Behold thy King cometh to thee, meek."**
**~ St. Matthew (21:5)**

**Thought:** The daughter of Sion is the soul. Jesus, in order to take possession of our souls, rides triumphantly first upon the ass and then upon the colt – that is, He becomes King of our hearts after having corrected us of our bad habits and our passions, which are here represented by the ass and the colt. How easily will He not effect His entry into our soul, now that it is no longer open to revolt and insubordination.

**Prayer:** Jesus, conquer my pride and my inertness. One word from Thee could work wonders in me.

**Practice:** Give yourself up to the government of Jesus.

ಜಲಜ❀ಚಲಚ

## 159 ~ Thursday

**"And the disciples going did as Jesus commanded them." ~ St. Matthew (21:6)**

**Thought:** The power of man lies in obedience. God speaks, let us act; God commands, let us do as we are commanded. This straightforward open simplicity is of itself strong enough to overturn all obstacles. It is simply heroic; this entire forgetfulness of self is super-human, yes, it is supernatural. It is no longer man who acts, judges, performs, but it is God who judges, acts, performs in him. Man acts according to the will of God; he does all things according to God's will and through His power.

**Prayer:** Jesus, be Thou my wisdom, my goodness, my power. When shall I become as a simple tool, obedient to Thy hand?

**Practice:** Yield an upright, simple, prompt, and blind obedience.

ಜಲಜ❀ಚಲಚ

**"And a very great multitude spread their garments in the way."** ~ St. Matthew (21:8)

**Thought:** Let us by spreading our inclinations before the feet of Jesus and submitting them to Him, welcome Him in His entry into our hearts. Let all our intentions and desires be under His direction. Let us also throw before Him branches of trees, palms, and leaves, typical of our triumph over our defects.

**Prayer:** Jesus, come as conqueror into my heart, and reign there over all my sense and faculties.

**Practice:** Leave all that concerns you in the hands of Jesus.

৩৩৩ ✠ ৩৩৩

# 161 ~Saturday

## "Hosanna to the Son of David."
## ~ St. Matthew (21:9)

**Thought**: Today hosannas ring through the air; all is glory and honour. Tomorrow it is "Crucify Him, crucify Him!" Such is the world! Such is mankind! Such is the sovereign at whose feet fools beg and scrape! Do you still trust the esteem and praise of the world?

**Prayer:** Jesus, Thou alone art my King and Saviour. Thou alone wilt be my Judge. What need have I of the opinion of men?

**Practice:** Despise the world's praises, as well as its condemnation.

ಖಖ✿ಲಲ

ಐಐ✤ಐಐಐಐ✤ಐಐಐಐ✤ಐಐ

## Paschal Tide

ಐಐ✤ಐಐಐಐ✤ಐಐಐಐ✤ಐಐ

### 162 ~ Easter Sunday

"And when the Sabbath was past, Mary Magdalen and Mary the mother of James and Salome bought sweet spices, that coming they might anoint Jesus." ~ St. Mark (16:1)

**Thought**: Primary devotion should consist in observance of the law. The holy women waited until the Sabbath was over to buy the sweet spices wherewith to anoint Jesus. But let us fulfil more than the precept requires, and when it is a question of honouring Jesus in His Body which is the Church, and in the members of His Body which are the poor, let us spare neither money nor labour.

**Prayer:** Jesus, if my love for Thee is real, I shall never think I have done enough to honour Thee.

**Practice:** Be zealous for the honour of the Church, and for the relief of the poor.

ಖಜಂ✦ಂ೪ಐ

## 163 ~ Monday

**"And very early in the morning the first day of the week, they come to the sepulchre, the sun being now risen." ~ St. Mark (16:2)**

**Thought:** Love is active, and prudent. Active – *valde mane*, they came very early in the morning. Hindrance or delay is unknown to those who love when it is a question of honouring the beloved. Prudent – *orto jam sole*, they came after the sun had risen. Love waits for the light; in spite of its ardour, it follows that natural sun given to us by God to guide us, namely, reason and faith, and also that supernatural sun whose brilliancy God gives us in addition to reason.

**Prayer:** Jesus, Sun of Truth for the intellect, Sun of Justice for the will, draw me towards Thee, grant that I may ever incline towards Thee, enlighten me, that I may always walk in the light of Thy word.

**Practice:** Be prudent and active in God's service.

ಖಜಂ✦ಂ೪ಐ

## 164 ~ Tuesday

**"Who shall roll us back the stone from the door of the sepulchre?"** ~ St. Mark (16:3)

**Thought:** How would it be if we were to know everything? Not only does an enormous stone close the entrance to the sepulchre, but this stone is sealed by the powerful enemies of Our Lord and is surrounded by soldiers. Go on in spite of all this; God asks of you only that which you are able to perform; He takes what seems impossible upon Himself. When you draw near, all these obstacles have disappeared. True, your sweet spices are of no service, but your wishes have been accomplished and even surpassed.

**Prayer:** Jesus, if Thou triest Thy friends, it is but to surprise them with consolations which more than recompense for any sacrifice.

**Practise:** Make progress in spite of obstacles.

౭౦౪౧౩౦౪౬

## 165 ~ Wednesday

**"And looking, they saw the stone rolled back."** ~ St. Mark (16:4)

**Thought:** When it is question of the honour of Our Lord, we should always go on. Obstacles that present themselves may be unconquerable for you; but God will send His Angel, and when you have done all that is in your power you will find the obstacle removed.

**Prayer:**   Jesus, give me effective love which nothing can ever quench, which will cause me to forget myself in the thought of Thee.

**Practice:**  Be constant in your efforts and trust God.

ಜುಖ❀ಲಿಲ

### 166 ~ Thursday

**"And entering into the sepulchre, they saw a young man sitting on the right side clothes with a white robe." ~ St. Mark (16:5)**

**Thought:**   When we have exhausted our wisdom and power, God sends us His Angels to enlighten and help us.  Thus anxiety is followed by a calm.  The Angel is sitting – *viderunt juvenem sedentem.*  Light follows darkness.  The Angel is clothed with a shining robe – *coopertum stola candida.*

**Prayer:** Jesus, I will ever continue in my search for Thee even in the shades of death, and by dint of searching I shall find light and peace.

**Practice**: Have Jesus ever in sight.

ಜುಖ❀ಲಿಲ

## 167 ~ Friday

**"Ye seek Jesus of Nazareth, who was crucified: He is risen, He is not here."**
**~ St. Mark (16:6)**

**Thought:** The Crucified One is risen again. Nailed upon the Cross, He was taunted by the Jews who defied Him to descend. He wished to surprise you – it was difficult to come down from the Cross whereon the Body was nailed hand and foot, but it was still more difficult to come out of the grave and return from death to life. Come now, ye enemies of Jesus, and shake your heads before this empty sepulchre – *surrexit, non est hic*, "He is risen, He is not here."

**Prayer:** Jesus, I will seek Thee crucified, and I shall find Thee risen and triumphant.

**Practice:** Be not afraid of the Cross of Christ.

ಖಖ⊛ಞಜ

## 168 ~ Saturday

**"But go, tell His disciples and Peter, that He goeth before you into Galilee."**
**~ St. Mark (16:7)**

**Thought:** All His disciples have abandoned Him, Peter has denied Him thrice, and Jesus holds great consolation in store for them, especially for him who is most guilty. Be not discouraged at your weakness and cowardice. Jesus is ready to forget all your misery. He will think only of your love and repentance. He anticipated you by the grace of calling you to Him; He again anticipates you by the grace of forgiveness – *proecedet vos in Galilaeam.*

**Prayer:** Jesus, in the day of battle thou didst remain alone; in the days of Thy triumph thou wert all-sufficient to Thyself, but Thou givest a share in Thy glory to those who had not the courage to share Thy sufferings and Thy ignominy.

**Practice:** No matter how unfaithful you may have been, be not discouraged.

ಐಐ❀ಐಐಐಐ❀ಐಐಐಐ❀ಐಐ

## 169 ~ First Sunday After Easter
## Divine Mercy Sunday

**"Now when it was late, and the doors were shut, Jesus came and stood in the midst, and said to them, Peace be to you."**
**~ St. John (20:19)**

**Thought:** The littleness of our faith retards the coming of Jesus; but when He sees that we really love Him He is not long in taking pity on our weakness. Besides, there is nothing to prevent Him – neither night, which He dissipates by the brightness of His glory, nor the door of our heart, which is no longer closed by mistrust and by fear. He can enter when He likes and as He likes.

**Prayer:**  Jesus, enter into my soul.  Thou alone canst establish there true calm and peace.

**Practice:** Have Jesus always present in your heart.

ಬಿಲ್ಲ ❀ ಲ್ಯ೦

## 170 ~ Monday

### "As the Father hath sent Me, I also send you." ~ St. John (20:21)

**Thought:**  The priest is God's ambassador – what a dignity!  The Angel said, "I shall be like unto the All High."  The All High is Jesus – *Tu solus altissimus Jesus Christe.*  The priest is the ambassador, the representative of Jesus Christ, as Jesus Christ Himself is the Word and image of the Heavenly Father.  Let honour and respect be paid to the priest who takes the place of the Most High!  Let honour be given to the Most High present in the priest.

**Prayer:**  Jesus, grant that the faithful may respect Thy minister and the minister may respect himself, so that while sustaining his dignity by word and deed, he may cause Thee to be respected in his person.

**Practice:** Respect for God's ministers.

ಬಿಲ್ಲ ❀ ಲ್ಯ೦

## 171 ~ Tuesday

**"Receive ye the Holy Ghost. Whose sins you shall forgive, they are forgiven; and whose sins you shall retain, they are retained."**
**~ St. John (20: 22-23)**

**Thought:** The Holy Ghost is given to the Apostles and by them is transmitted to the priest, who can give or hold back grace, who has power of forgiving or retaining sins. Thus it is that the sinner receives absolution with moral assurance of pardon and reconciliation.

**Prayer:** I thank Thee for the power granted by Thee to Thy ministers to save me.

**Practice:** Frequent and earnest confession.

బుజన ✸ ఇలుబ

## 172 ~ Wednesday

**"We have seen the Lord. ... Except I shall see ... I will not believe." ~ St. John (20:25)**

**Thought:** The Apostles rejected the testimony of the holy women. Thomas refuses their testimony. This is justice,[4] and Thomas is consistent. And yet

---

4    Not that he was just in disbelieving their testimony, but acting justly in being prudent with regards to extraordinary reports of the supernatural. Fr. de Boylesve uses this as an example to show it is

what rashness in this same prudence, which dares to impose conditions upon our God. Certainly we must be prudent. We must not look upon the first idea crossing our imagination as an inspiration from on high, but we must not exact from God additional miracles and the revelation of Himself to us. To determine our belief in what God has affirmed, and to act according to His wishes, it should suffice that the light of reason, and the authority of wise and sincere men, discover to us the revelation which has already been made.

**Prayer:** Jesus, I am in total darkness; but if Thou dost not enlighten me at once, I will be guided by those whom Thou hast chosen for me as my superiors.

**Practice:** Practice docility, the wise medium between foolish credulity which believes in everything, and brutal stubbornness which believes in nothing.

ଧଃ୬୭❀ଔ୬ଔ

---

good to be prudent and test every inspiration for not all of our first ideas are heaven-sent inspirations, and yet, we must not be rash to constantly demand miracles or extraordinary signs from God to show us the way. Fr. de Boylesve also shows St. Thomas was rash in this area as he demanded an extraordinary sign as proof of the testimony of the apostles and the holy women. In this case, Fr. de Boylesve notes we should not test God or put conditions on Him to show Himself, but we must rely on the lights of faith and reason, and also the authority given to those wise people whom God has sent us to affirm what has already been revealed by Him concerning His will and teachings.

# 173 ~ Thursday

## "Be not faithless, but believing."
## ~ St. John (20:27)

**Thought:** Docility is a better proof of intelligence than incredulity. What is required to refuse belief? Obstinacy, than which nothing is easier – one need only refrain from exercising his intelligence. What must one do to believe? One must listen attentively with the desire of being instructed. Docility most facilitates instruction. Incredulity is a refusal to listen or learn, a brutal persistence in ignorance. The incredulous man is a being confined in the sphere of his own mind.

**Prayer:** Jesus, faith is as much a gift as intelligence – the latter a natural, the former a supernatural gift. Thou hast given me both – the former in creating me, the latter in making me a Christian. Give me, O Jesus, an increase of both.

**Practice:** Firmness of faith.

ಖಐ❀ಛಾಚಕ

## 174 ~ Friday

### "My Lord, and my God." ~ St. John (20:28)

**Thought:** Thomas, whose belief was more slow than that of the others, surpasses them all in his protestation of belief. No one until now had so openly declared the Divinity of Jesus Christ. Let us never say, Oh! It is too late; but, by renewal of our efforts, let us make up for hesitation or for loss of time.

**Prayer:** Jesus, I submit. Thy resurrection proves to me Thy power; the marks of Thy wounds prove Thy bounty towards me. Thou art my Lord, and my God.

**Practice:** Zeal in making up for your negligence in the past.

ಠಞ❀ಞಐ

## 175 ~ Saturday

### "Blessed are they that have not seen and have believed." ~ St. John (20:29)

**Thought:** Readiness of belief may be a sign of a weak or a strong mind – a weak mind inasmuch as one through sloth or wantonness finds it easy to believe what comes first to hand: a strong-minded one inasmuch as having compared the statements of witnesses and the proofs of their doctrine, one believes in their words at once. Narrow minds argue incessantly and cavil at everything that is said.

**Prayer:** Jesus, I believe. Thy Divinity is amply and sufficiently proved. Speak, then; I will believe all Thou tellest me – every word spoken by Thy mouth.

**Practice:** Do not reason so much. God has spoken – believe.

ಜಬಾ❀ಲ೮ಜಬಾಜಾ❀ಲ೮ಜಬಾಜಾ❀ಲ೮ಜ

## 176 ~ The Second Sunday After Easter

### "I am the good Shepherd." ~ St. John (10:11)

**Thought:** The Good Shepherd directs, feeds, and defends His flock. Jesus directs us by His word and example, feeds us with His Body and Blood in the Eucharist, and defends us by His Cross against our enemies, which are the world, the flesh, and the devil.

**Prayer:** Jesus, give me the meekness and confidence of the sheep – meekness, that I may be wholly guided by Thee; confidence, that I may seek Thee when I am attacked by the enemy.

**Practice:** Imitate Jesus, His doctrines and His example.

ಜಬಾ❀ಲ೮ಜ

"**The Good Shepherd giveth His life for the sheep.**" ~ St. John (10:11)

**Thought:** Let us realise what is the price of a soul. It is worthy Jesus Christ's own life. Jesus is Wisdom itself; He would not give His life for a soul if the soul were unworthy of the sacrifice; and if such is the value of my soul, the value of my brother's soul is as great. I must then do everything in my power for the salvation of my neighbour.

**Prayer:** Jesus, give me courage to sacrifice all things for the salvation firstly of my own soul, and secondly, for that of my neighbour.

**Practice:** Live and die for the salvation of souls.

ಐಐ⊛ಞಚ

178 ~ **Tuesday**

"**But the hireling seeth the wolf coming, and leaveth the sheep and flieth.**"
~ St. John (10:13)

**Thought:** The wolf represents the heretic, sophist, the man of scandal, or any one who by word or example would draw the Christian into error or vice. Unless you fight against error and vice you are a hireling; you have no love for souls, nor for Jesus

Christ who has redeemed souls by His own Blood. What, then, would you be if you were to demand freedom for error and vice?

**Prayer:**   Jesus, inspire me with a constant hatred and a holy anger against error and vice.

**Practice:**   Think often of Jesus, who is ever thinking of you.

ಖ಼ಖ಼❀ಚಚಚ

## 179 ~ Wednesday

**"I know Mine (sheep), and Mine know me." ~ St. John (10:14)**

**Thought:**   If I were to say to you, The Pope has spoken of you, you would exclaim, What! Does the Pope know me? It is very likely that the Pope knows you not; but it is very certain that Jesus knows you, thinks of you, and is preparing for you a place in His heavenly fold. And you, do you know Him? You know full well that He became man and died for you. Do you think of it?

**Prayer:**   Jesus, teach me to know Thee and think of Thee, and like the sheep, ever to look up to Thee for guidance.

**Practice**:   Often think of Jesus, Who is ever thinking of you.

ಖ಼ಖ಼❀ಚಚಚ

"As the Father knoweth Me, and I know the Father; and I lay down My life for My sheep." ~ St. John (10:15)

**Thought:** The infinite love which the Father and Son have for each other proceeds from that mutual understanding existing between Them. So from the mutual understanding of Shepherd and sheep springs a love which induces the Shepherd to give His life for His sheep, the sheep to sacrifice their life for their Shepherd. Jesus Christ dies for Christians, and Christians die martyrs for Jesus Christ. All understanding which does not tend towards love is sterile and useless; love which is not ready for action is false and imaginary. Now the effect of love is the abandonment and sacrifice of one's self.

**Prayer:** Jesus, what didst Thou see in me worthy of Thy life's sacrifice? Thou didst see the image of Thy Father and Thyself, for Thou art the Image of the Father. Thus Thou does recognise and love in me, both Thy Father and Thyself.

**Practice:** Sacrifice yourself for souls and for Jesus.

ಔಙಾ✦ಂಙಶ

## 181 ~ Friday

**"And other sheep I have that are not of this fold."** ~ St. John (10:16)

**Thought:** I am one of those sheep whom Jesus had in His mind then. What can I do to respond to His solicitude and tenderness? Firstly, I will be docile to His call and will faithfully follow Him; secondly, I will share His solicitude and will endeavour to lead to Him those other sheep belonging to Him whom He wishes to save, but who are being lost outside His fold.

**Prayer:** Jesus, Thou are the only Shepherd, Thou alone givest souls their nourishment, which is truth for the mind and justice for the will.

**Practice:** Pray, and if in your power, give something towards the propagation of the Faith.

ಬಂಜಂ ❀ ಆಲ

## 182 ~ Saturday

**"And there shall be one fold and one Shepherd."** ~ St. John. (10:16)

**Thought:** Jesus is the one Shepherd. The Vicar of Christ is the one shepherd, one and the same with Jesus Christ. Let us believe in what Christ teaches and in what He proclaims by the mouth of His Vicar, and we shall have one and the same mind, one and the same belief.  Let us desire what God desires and commands through His representative here on earth, and we shall have one and the same will, one and the same heart.  Then there will but one fold and One Shepherd.

**Prayer:** Jesus, I believe all that Thou teachest, I desire all that Thou commandest.

**Practice:** Faith, and obedience to Christ and His Vicar.

ಜಿಞ ✸ ಐಲ಼ಜಿಞ ✸ ಐಲ಼ಜಿಞ ✸ ಐಲ಼

## 183 ~ Third Sunday After Easter

### "A little while and now you shall not see Me." ~ St. John (16:16)

**Thought:** Jesus often conceals His presence from the faithful soul and permits her to suffer without light or consolation.  But He always forewarns her, and grants her enough light and strength to guide and fortify her during the trial.

**Prayer:** Jesus, if it is Thy wish to prove me and to conceal Thyself from me, do not be far off, but in Thy concealment still be present to me.

**Practice:** Confide in Jesus, even when He may seemingly be absent.

ಜಿಞ ✸ ಐಲ಼

184

## 184 ~ Monday

## "And again a little while, and you shall see Me."
## ~ St. John (16:16)

**Thought:** After day comes night, and after night comes day. Trial follows consolation, consolation follows trial; *Modicum*, a little while, consolation but a short while - *et iterum modicum*, desolation, too, is of short duration. Let us take advantage of the time of consolation to direct our course and to be in readiness when the tempest shall burst forth. Let us profit by desolation and recognise our weakness, let us humble ourselves to discover what is wanting in us. During time of consolation the remembrance of our weakness should keep us humble; and when desolation is upon us, the knowledge of its short duration should sustain and strengthen us.

**Prayer:** Jesus, from Thy hands only do I expect that peace which can never be obtained from man.

**Practice:** Hope always, but in Jesus only.

ಋಞ⊕ಞಠ

## 185 ~ Tuesday

**"Because I go to My Father." ~ St. John (16:16)**

**Thought:** Wherefore this disappearance of Our Lord? Because He returns to His Father. Why does He return? – *Vado parare vobis locum.* We shall see Him again. He will return to judge and reward us; let us rejoice at His absence. It is to your interest and will only last a short while. Let us rejoice at it for His sake. He returns to His Father to enjoy that glory He has so well deserved.

**Prayer:** Jesus, go unto Thy Father and associate Thy holy humanity with the glory of Thy Divinity, but do not forget me, who am the least member of that great Body which is Thine own – viz., the Holy Church.

**Practice:** Union with the Father through Jesus Christ.

ಜಞ✤ಲಇಚ

## 186 ~ Wednesday

**"We know not what He speaketh."**
**~ St. John (16:18)**

**Thought:** Often I do not know what God wishes to tell me, especially when I meet with contradiction; and yet contradiction is a word of God as clear and as efficacious as any of God's words. Opposition often contributes more largely than favour towards the perfection of a work undertaken for the glory of God.

**Prayer:** Jesus, Thou abandonest me just at the moment of action. This desertion would be inexplicable if it were real; but it is only apparent. From heaven above where Thou sittest in Thy glory, and from the depths of my heart where Thou dwellest by grace, Thou never ceasest to enlighten and strengthen me.

**Practice:** Constancy in the darkness of trial.

ಖಾ⚕ೞ

## 187 ~ Thursday

### "Your sorrow shall be changed into joy."
### ~ St. John (16:20)

**Thought:** Even upon earth in my lifetime, if I place all my hope in Jesus, and in Jesus only, joy will succeed to sadness, or rather sadness itself will be changed into joy; that which was sorrow will turn into happiness. The trial which I looked upon as an evil will become the source of good.

**Prayer:** Jesus, sustain me still in times of trial, for without Thy help I cannot await Thy return.

**Practice:** Always hope, even against hope.

ಐಐ✿ಐಐ

## 188 ~ Friday

**"I will see you again, and your heart will rejoice." ~ St. John (16:22)**

**Thought:** Everything is not lost when Jesus conceals Himself. He disappears only to return. The sun is no further from the earth during the night than during the day, nor does it cause the earth to move more slowly when there is darkness. Besides, be patient; joy that follows trial is more true and more pure.

**Prayer:** Jesus, if I love Thee as I ought, that is, more than myself – if forgetting self I seek only for Thee, I shall be like to Thee, ever happy.

**Practise:** Rejoice at the glory of God.

ಐಐ✿ಐಐ

## 189 ~ Saturday

**"And your joy no man shall take from you."**
**~ St. John (16:22)**

**Thought:** Jesus alone can give that joy which neither world nor death can steal away from us. We must free ourselves of everything which pertains not to Jesus Christ. Willingly or unwillingly we shall have one day to give up and sacrifice everything – Jesus alone will remain to us.

**Prayer:** Jesus, give me to understand and feel that Thou alone art sufficient for me, and that without Thee al the world is as nothing.

**Practice:** Rejoice in Jesus, and through Jesus only.

ಜುಜಾ ❀ ಇಚಳಜುಜಾ ❀ ಇಚಳಜುಜಾ ❀ ಇಚಳ

## 190 ~Fourth Sunday After Easter

### "And now I go to Him that sent Me."
### ~ St. John (16:5)

**Thought:** Go, Lord; go, give an account of Thy mission – Thy hands and feet pierced by nails, Thy Heart pierced, tell plainly how Thou hast fulfilled Thy mission. Immortal glory awaiteth Thee!

**Prayer:** Jesus, Thou in turn has sent me. But what have I done? Where are the marks of self-sacrifice? Where are the souls I should offer to Thee?

**Practice:** Faithfulness to the duties of your vocation.

ಜುಜಾ ❀ ಇಚಳ

## 191 ~ Monday

**"It is expedient to you that I go."**
**~ St. John (16:7)**

**Thought:** The devotion which we know we feel – sensible devotion – is useful; but it is also useful and important that we should be deprived of it. It behoves us to know what we are, and what is our worth when Jesus takes away from us His visible help. Then must that sensible devotion give place to the truly spiritual devotion; Jesus must be concealed that He may send us His Spirit, which is the Holy Ghost.

**Prayer:** Jesus, if Thou takest from me Thy sensible presence, do not withdraw Thy aid from me; without Thee I can do nothing.

**Practice:** Rely always upon Jesus, whether He be manifest or hidden.

ಐಐ✿ಲಲ

## 192 ~ Tuesday

**"If I go not, the Paraclete will not come to you."**
**~ St. John (16:7)**

**Thought:** The Apostles must forfeit the legitimate and pure satisfaction which they feel in enjoying the visible presence of Jesus Christ, and I am desirous of enjoying both the world and God! I would unite and keep in my heart the spirit of the world and the spirit of Jesus!

**Prayer:** Jesus, draw me away from all worldly things. Then with the help of the Holy Ghost I shall be raised up to Thee.

**Practice:** Detach yourself from all that is sensible, even from sensible devotion.

ಬಿ‍ಫಿ❀ಲ‍ಞ

### 193 ~ Wednesday

**"He will convince the world of sin, and of justice, and of judgement." ~ St. John (16:8)**

**Thought:** The world sinned when it crucified Jesus Christ. It will be convinced of its sin when Jesus by His resurrection shall prove Himself to be the Just One. Then also will the world be judged and found guilty of Deicide. This judgement hangs over all those who refuse submission to Jesus Christ.

**Prayer:** Jesus, Thou art my God, my Saviour, and my King; I submit to Thy word and to Thy guidance.

**Practice:** Confidence in Jesus, the Conqueror of the world.

ಬಿ‍ಫಿ❀ಲ‍ಞ

## 194 ~ Thursday

**"He will teach you all truth." ~ St. John (16:13)**

**Thought:** The Holy Ghost is the first of teachers. Let us listen to Him when He speaks inwardly by secret inspiration, or outwardly by the voice of the Church. There is no truth at all useful for the salvation and true happiness of the soul which is not surely and fully taught by the Holy Ghost.

**Prayer:** Jesus, in Thy Gospel, and especially by Thy example, Thy has said that Thou dost teach all useful truth; but without the Holy Ghost I should understand neither Thy word nor Thy example.

**Practice:** Frequently invoke the Holy Ghost.

ಐಖಾ✾ೞೞ

## 195 ~ Friday

**"He shall glorify Me." ~ St. John (16:14)**

**Thought:** The Holy Ghost shall glorify Jesus! How? By teaching me to know Jesus, and by persuading me to follow Him. By understanding His doctrine I shall recognise His wisdom; in imitating His example I shall make manifest His virtue.

**Prayer:** Jesus, fill me with Thy Spirit that I may glorify Thee, make Thee known and praised, and cause Thee to be loved and served.

**Practice:** In all things seek the glory of Jesus.

ಜಐ❀ಞಚ

## 196 ~ Saturday

**"All things whatsoever the Father hath are Mine." ~ St. John (16:15)**

**Thought:** Everything belongs equally to Father, Son, and Holy Ghost. Now the Father has given us the Son, and the Father and the Son have given us the Holy Ghost. All that the Father has, then, is ours. True, we do not as yet enjoy these things; we are like the heir who possesses only the title-deeds which constitute him owner of the domain of which he has not yet the use. Let us keep these deeds and keep the grace of God, and our happiness is certain.

**Prayer:** Jesus, keep me, or rather keep Thyself in me, either by Communion, which maketh Thee to live in me and me in Thee, or by the grace of Thy Holy Ghost, which gives me life from Thee, by Thee, and for Thee.

**Practice:** Union with God the Father by Jesus Christ in the Holy Ghost.

ಜಐ❀ಞಚ

ಶುಭ ✿ ಲೇಉ಼ಶುಭ ✿ ಲೇಉ಼ಶುಭ ✿ ಲೇಉ಼

## 197 ~ Fifth Sunday After Easter

**"If you ask the Father anything in My Name, He will give it to you." ~ St. John (16:23)**

**Thought:** This is a formal promise. Who will doubt it? "Anything you ask" *Si quid*. Nothing is withheld, neither spiritual nor temporal blessings. Why, then, do you ask so seldom and for so little? You are in want of so many things, and it is so easy to obtain them.

**Prayer:** Jesus, what a Name is Thine! What power in Thy Name alone! I wish it to be ever in my heart and always on my lips. By Thy Name I can do everything; in the Name and for the Name of Jesus I desire everything.

**Practice:** Pray incessantly, and ask everything in the Name of Jesus.

ಶುಭ ✿ ಲೇಉ಼

## 198 ~ Monday

**"Ask, and you shall receive, that your joy may be made full. ~ St. John (16:24)**

**Thought:** Nothing rejoices the soul so much as prayer. Ask, you shall receive more than you have desired. Thus shall your joy be made full. Pray, and experience will tell you that God is good and powerful.

**Prayer:** Jesus, why should I not always ask? Thy only wish is to give.

**Practice:** Pray continually.

ಜುಙ⊕ಞ౮ಙ

## 199 ~ Tuesday

### "I will show you plainly of the Father."
### ~ St. (John 16:25)

**Thought:** Jesus is always speaking to us of His Father - "word of the Father", "image of the Father", "brightness of the Father"; His office is to manifest the Father. But He often speaks to us in hidden terms. He shows us the Father to us as He is in His works. Let us pray, and He will show the Father to us as He is in Himself. Then seeing God face to face, we shall be like unto Him, happy in His happiness, glorious in His glory.

**Prayer:** Jesus, grant that all interior and exterior words of mine may be like Thee, the Word of God; may they serve as a connecting link between the Father and me by the purity, uprightness, and divinity of intention.

**Practice:** Do all things for the love of God only.

ಜುಙ⊕ಞ౮ಙ

## 200 ~ Wednesday

**"The Father Himself loveth you, because you have loved Me." ~ St. John (16:27)**

**Thought:** To love Jesus is to love the Son of God; to love the Son is to love the Father, for the Son should be loved solely because He is one and the same with the Father. How could the Father refuse love to Him by whom He is beloved? Besides, he that loves the Son loves Him whom the Father loves. So does the Father love you because you love His Beloved.

**Prayer:** Jesus, be Thou the centre of all my affections. In loving Thee I shall love the Father, the Blessed Virgin Thy Mother and Thy brethren, for if I love Thee I shall love those who are like Thee, who are loved by Thee, and who in turn love Thee too.

**Practice:** Have Jesus ever in your hearts.

ಜ೫ಲ෧෪෪෨

## 201 ~ Ascension Thursday

**"I came forth from the Father, and am come into the world." ~ St. John (16:28)**

**Thought:** Jesus never left His Father, was never separated from Him; but He came from the Father into this world just as the interior word comes forth from the soul in order to be heard in the world and spread about, thus becoming exterior though still dwelling in the soul. In speaking, my words gain both the ear and the intelligence of those who listen and understand me, and yet still remain in me who speak and think. Thus the Incarnate Word of God is at one and the same time in God, of whom He is the Word, and in the world to which He shows Himself.

**Prayer:** Jesus, grant that like Thee I may come from the Father, that like Thee I may be able by my word to enlighten souls.

**Practice:** Be united to God in all your outward actions.

ಬಲಾ⊛ೞಲ

## 202 ~ Friday

### "Again I leave the world, and go to the Father." ~ St. John (16:28)

**Thought:** To follow the example of Jesus I must by means of prayer detach myself from the world and look up to God. As the Man-God, so the man of God runs his course; from God He comes down into the world and from the world He goes back to God. From prayer He descends to good works, from good works He returns to prayer. Love of God engenders love of our neighbour who is the image of God, and the love of our neighbour reflects the love of God.

**Prayer**: Jesus, Thou dost leave the world both for Thyself and for us. For Thyself, that Thou mayest find again Thy splendour and Thy glory in the Father; for us, to prepare for us a place beside Thy Father.

**Practice:** Raise up your mind by constant prayer to God.

ಜಙಾ✵ಞಲ

### 203 ~ Saturday

## "Now we know that Thou knowest all things." ~ St. John (16:30)

**Thought:** Thou dost read our hearts and minds; Thou answerest our demands, our desires, before even they are expressed. Thus we know that Thou knowest all things. Thou not only knowest but canst accomplish all things, Thy only wish is for our good; I will then place all my confidence in Thee.

**Prayer:** Jesus, Thou knowest my desires; but what is better, Thou knowest what is fit and needful for me. If my desires are not in keeping with my wants, if what I ask of Thee is not proper, correct my desires and my petitions, give me only what I stand in need of to serve and glorify Thee.

**Practice:** Place the accomplishment of your desires in the hands of Jesus.

ಜಙಾ✵ಞಲ

ಜುಕ⊕ ಡುೞಜುಕ⊕ ಡುೞಜುಕ⊕ ಡುೞ

## 204 ~ Sunday (The Ascension)

*N.B. ~ We would here propose as meditation for the seven days following this feast the Gospel of the Ascension, but give, nevertheless, seven meditations upon the Gospel of the Sunday within the Octave of the Ascension.[5]*

**"Go ye into the whole world and preach the Gospel to every creature."**
**~ St. Mark (16: 15)**

**Thought:** How can I go into the whole world? By prayer and good works. We must pray for all mankind, for all nations, for Christians and infidels, for the sinful and the wicked as well as for the just, for the dead, the dying, and the living. Let each one speak according to his condition, in private and in public, let us speak by word and by writing, announcing Jesus to every creature, to the impious and to the cold of heart, as much as and even more than to the faithful and the fervent Christian - *omni creaturae*. Prayer is never offered in vain, and words spoken are never lost: if good, they do good; if evil, they do harm.

**Prayer:** Jesus, my sole, or at least my chief thought must be to make Thee known to those who know Thee not, to instil the love of Thee in the minds of those who neither serve nor know Thee. Grant Thou

---

5        Here is where Fr. de Boylesve offers an additional or alternative set of meditations for the week around the feast of the Ascension. See the Table of Contents.

my prayer; give eloquence to my tongue, that both the one and the other may be efficaciously used in Thy service.

**Practice:** Spread wide Christian doctrine by preaching and in conversation, by the propagation of good books if you are able; if not, by the propagation of religious works.

ꕔꕪ❀ꕉꕪ

## 205 ~ Monday

**"He that believeth, and is baptised, shall be saved." ~ St. Mark (16:16)**

**Thought:** It is not sufficient to believe; we must be baptised and must observe the law. But baptism and observance of the law are not sufficient; we must, besides, have belief. Neither faith without goods works, nor good works without faith, can lead us to salvation. Nor can I without God save myself, nor will God save me without my co-operation. God offers me His grace in vain; unless I accept it I can never profit by His help. In vain He draws me to Him; unless I make the step towards Him I shall never reach. In vain does He give Himself to me if I, on my part, do not receive Him. How can I possess Him if I do not unite myself to Him?

**Prayer:** Jesus, give me light and strength – light by faith and by Thy Divine Word, strength by baptism, which fills me with Thy grace.

**Practice:** Believe and act.

ಬಾಬಾ ⊛ ಅಬ

## 206 ~ Tuesday

### "In My Name they shall cast out devils."
### ~ St. Mark (16:17)

**Thought:** Let us fathom our power as Christians and learn how to use it. By a single word we may cast out *devils*, and still more easily may we cast out those human agents who are much less powerful than the infernal spirits. Why is not the grand and holy name of Jesus ever on our lips and in our hearts?

**Prayer:** Jesus, grant that in moments of temptation Thy blessed Name may be upon my lips.

**Practice:** Oftentimes invoke the holy Name of Jesus.

ಬಾಬಾ ⊛ ಅಬ

## 207 ~ Wednesday

### "They shall speak with new tongues."
### ~ St. Mark (16:17)

**Thought:** Are you desirous of knowing if you have really received the Holy Ghost? Do you speak a new tongue? If you live in a worldly frame of mind, you are heard to praise riches, pleasures, honours. If you live in the Holy Ghost, your language will be different. You will praise poverty, suffering, abjection, and all that the world despises. You will despise what is praised by the world, passing wealth, sensual pleasure, worldly glory.

**Prayer:** Jesus, teach me to speak like Thee and for this end teach me Thy tongue, give me the language of Thy example, of Thy lessons, of Thy Gospel, and of Thy Cross.

**Practice:** Judge not nor speak according to the ideas of the world.

ಖಖ⊛ಐಬ

## 208 ~ Ascension Thursday

**"And the Lord Jesus, after He had spoken to them, was taken up into heaven, and sitteth on the right hand of God," ~ St. Mark (16:19)**

**Thought:** Yesterday Jesus was nailed upon the Cross and His enemies defied Him to descend; today He ascends into Heaven. Could they prevent His ascent, and thus prevent His coming down to judge us. Yesterday Jesus was suspended by three nails betwixt heaven and earth; today He is sitting tranquilly on the right hand of His Father. After humiliation comes glory, after labour comes repose, after suffering there is joy.

**Prayer:** Jesus, from the right hand of Thy Father where Thou sittest Thou dost descend each day, each instant, upon our altars; Thou dost come down into our hearts, to make of Thy Church and of all of us one great Body, whose head shall reach to the highest heavens.

**Practice:** Dwell in Heaven in thought, desire, faith, and hope.

ಋಞ✠ಐಉ

## 209 ~ Friday

**"And they (the Apostles), going forth, preached everywhere. ~ St. Mark (16:20)**

**Thought:** If you love Jesus you will not stand motionless, gazing at that point in the heavens where He disappeared from your sight. You will go forth into the world and make Him known and loved, causing Him to reign over all minds by faith, and over all hearts by charity. These is no repose here below. In Heaven we shall sit down with Jesus. Meanwhile, let us keep close to Jesus; let us advance continually, and never linger.

**Prayer:** Jesus, be with me according to Thy promise until the end of the world. Be with me until my last hour. Grant that by word, and still more by example, I may cause Thee to be known and loved.

**Practice:** Speak of Jesus continually and in all places, that He may be known and served by all.

ಋಞ✠ಐಉ

**"The Lord working withal, and confirming the word with signs that followed."**
**~ St. Mark (16:20)**

**Thought:** Unless the Lord works with you, your actions will profit nothing. If He approves not of your word by Divine recognition, it will not be accepted. Now what may be the signs of Divine co-operation and approval? Sometimes miracles in the physical order – for instance the curing of the sick, the resurrection of the dead; but more often miracles in the moral order, such as the conversion of sinners and the practice of heroic virtues. Jesus, in Thy Gospel Thou hast revealed to us Thy truth, but above all, by Thy example Thou hast taught us all things necessary.

**Prayer:** Jesus, help me to make Thee known and loved. Experience has shown me but too clearly how powerless I am without Thy aid.

**Practice:** Count upon Divine help only for success in good works, and yet labour and act as though success depended only upon your efforts.

ಬುಙ❀ಲ್ಞಚ

## 211 ~ <u>Sunday within the</u> <u>Octave of the Ascension</u>

**"But when the Paracelete cometh, whom I will send you from the Father, the Spirit of Truth who proceedeth from the Father, He shall give testimony of Me." ~ St. John (15:26)**

<u>**Thought:**</u> From whence springs that intellectual and moral superiority of the Christian over the most learned and upright pagan?   How is it that a child twelve years old knows more than the most sublime and most profound philosopher of pagan Greece about God and man, and of the connection between God and man?  According to the teachings of faith the Christian receives in baptism the Spirit of the Father and the Son, the Spirit of Truth, the Spirit of Sanctity.  Be cognisant of your superiority, and be not led by the spirit of the world.

<u>**Prayer:**</u>  Jesus, replenish in my soul the Spirit proceeding from Thee from Thy Father.  That alone can preserve me from the spirit of error and falsehood which governs the world; that alone can drive away the breath of corruption which covers the world.

<u>**Practice:**</u> Follow with docility the instructions and inspirations of the Holy Ghost.

ಖಕ⊛ಲಿಲು

# 212 ~ Monday

## "He shall give testimony of Me."
## ~ St. John (15:26)

**Thought:** Neither reason nor the senses can teach us to know Jesus Christ. The Holy Ghost alone discovers to us the Son of God in the Son of man. Are you desirous of converting the unbeliever and the impious, of awaking the Christian spirit in your own soul? Have recourse to the teaching of the Gospel and of the Church. The Holy Ghost inspired the Gospel, and He assists the Church. But above all, remember that faith is a gift. Pray, then, and invoke the Spirit of Light and Truth.

**Prayer:** Jesus, Thou hast explained to us Thy word. Thou hast sent us Thy Spirit. How can we resist this double testimony? My God, I do believe, but complete Thy work; and since Thy Spirit is not only the Spirit of Truth, but also the Spirit of Sanctity, grant through it that my life may be spent in conformity with Thy word, and my own belief.

**Practice:** Live like Jesus Christ, and you will live by the Holy Ghost.

৪৯৩❀৫৭৪

# 213 ~ Tuesday

**"And you shall give Me testimony, because you are with Me from the beginning."**
**~ St. John (15: 27)**

**Thought:** What honour for poor needy sinners, to be called to give testimony of Jesus Christ! Surely they who already have the testimony of the Holy Ghost need not that of nameless, worthless men. All the advantage is on their side. The names of these sinners will be more popular, more glorious, than the name of an Alexander or of a Plato. The glory rendered by them to Jesus Christ by the testimony of their word and blood comes back upon them and surrounds their memory with immortal glory.

**Prayer:** Jesus, I too have been with Thee from the first moments of my existence, from the hour of baptism. Grant that my life, still more than my words, may be a continual witness to the strength of Thy grace and of Thy example.

**Practice:** Have nothing at heart but the glory of Jesus Christ, you will then participate in the splendour of His glory.

ಬುಬಾ ❀ ಲ್ಲಚ

**"These things have I spoken to you, that you may not be scandalised."** ~ St. John (6:1)

**Thought:** Wherefore are you astonished at the tribulations which oppress the Church? Wherefore are you scandalised at the persecutions undergone by the Saints? Was not Jesus Christ hated and attacked by all? Was there any kind of suffering or infamy that He did not submit to? You say God abandons His Church, and delivers His own people to the enemy; so did He abandon His Beloved Son, delivering Him to a traitor, to insolent, cowardly judges, to the mob and to the rabble. But you must remember this trial lasted only a few hours, sufficiently long however to show forth the heroism of Charity, while the glory of His triumph shall last for ever and ever.

**Prayer:** Jesus, do not permit me to be scandalised at Thy Cross. It was a royal road to glory for Thee, and it cannot be a less royal road for Thy Church, for Thy Saints, and for myself.

**Practice:** Accept suffering and humiliation.

✺

## 215 ~ Thursday

**"The hour cometh, that whosoever killeth you will think that he doth a service to God."**
**~ St. John (16:2)**

**Thought:** And, indeed, in the name of the law, justice, and morality, for the good of nations, in the interests of religion, and for the honour of God's name, enemies to God and religion, men, lawless and immoral, proclaim far and wide the necessity of exiling and even of exterminating priests and religious – of rooting out all Christians who are distinguished by their opposition to error and vice. So, too, did Jesus suffer. In the name of the law, for the honour of God and for the benefit of the nation was He condemned as a blasphemer and seducer, and condemned to death.

**Prayer:** Jesus, give me the courage of a martyr. Our times and country still hold out to us the martyr's palm, which may seem to have belonged to the time of Nero, or to the countries of Tonquin and Korea.

**Practice:** Endure with patience those petty humiliations and sufferings of each day, and you will be prepared for great combats.

ಜಜಾ⊕ಞಚ

## 216 ~ Friday

"And these things they will do to you, because they have not known the Father nor Me." ~ **St. John** (16:3)

**Thought:** O Lord, they know Thee not. They know not that Thou art King and Master of the universe, and that they are thus unable to escape Thy judgement. They ignore both the Father and Thee. They will not recognise in Thee the Son of God, born to save the world. They understand not that in rejecting Thee they are lost forever. If they did not persist in ignoring Thee, they would readily receive Thy ambassadors; they would be governed and saved by Thy Church.

**Prayer:** Jesus, how can I complain that my intentions are misconstrued and aspersed, when I see how mankind ignores all that Thy Father has done in sending Thee to succour them, all that Thou hast done by Thy sacrifice upon the Cross, all Thou still doest by Thy sacrifice on our altars.

**Practice:** Do good, and expect nothing but forgetfulness and contempt from men.

೮೮೦ ✿ ೞೞ

"But these thing I have told you, that when the hour of them shall come, you may remember that I told you." ~ St. John (16:4)

**Thought:** Persecution teaches us two things – our weakness and our strength; our *weakness* in ourselves and by ourselves; a few wicked but hardened men can silence and frighten the good, and can even render them powerless: our *strength* in God and from God; for women and children with His help and grace, have despised the fury of the mob, the power of a Caesar.

**Prayer:** Jesus, Thou art not like the world, given to deceit. The world promises honours and pleasures, but gives only shame and remorse. Thou didst announce the Cross, and didst hold by Thy divine word. To the Cross Thou didst promise victory, and Thy saints are crowned with honour and glory.

**Practice:** In the midst of suffering and humiliation think of the glory awaiting you in heaven.

ಋಷಿ ❀ ಞಲಇ

༄༅། ❀ ༄༅། ❀ ༄༅། ❀ ༄༅།

## Pentecost

༄༅། ❀ ༄༅། ❀ ༄༅། ❀ ༄༅།

### 218 ~ Sunday

**"If any man love Me, he will keep My word." ~ St. John (14:24)**

**Thought:** Love consists in the union of the lover and the object loved. Intelligent beings are united by thought and will. Friends think alike, their desires are similar. If you love Jesus Christ you must think as He thinks, desire what He desires, do what He wishes; so you will keep His word, and do as He thinks, wishes, and desires. All other love is false.

**Prayer:** Jesus, grant me light to understand Thy word, and strength to accomplish it.

**Practice:** Follow strictly God's commandments, and the particular rules of your profession.

## 219 ~ Monday

### "And My Father will love him."
### ~ St. John (14:23)

**Thought:** What grace, what glory to be loved by God the Father! What must I do to obtain this honour? Jesus tells me I must love Him and follow His wishes, and do His bidding. "If any man loveth Me, he will keep My word, and My Father will love him." It is not here a question of sentiment or of sublime contemplation; it needs not a great heart nor an elevated understanding. Love Jesus, believe His word, obey His commandments; then will you be friend of the Father, Son, and Holy Ghost.

**Prayer:** Jesus Thy word suffices. It shall be my light and strength.

**Practice:** Cling to Jesus, by believing His doctrine and obeying His instructions.

ಹುಞಾ✿ಲ಴ಚ

## 220 ~ Tuesday

### "And We will come to him, and will make Our abode with him" ~ St. John (14: 23)

**Thought**: I cannot attain the height where God is, but I can believe what Jesus teaches and do what He commands. On these conditions will Father and Son come unto me. I may not dwell in God, but if I only

213

believe and accomplish the word of Jesus Christ, He will establish His dwelling in me.  I shall not be in heaven, but heaven will be in me, which imports the same.

**Prayer:** Jesus, come and dwell in me that I may dwell in Thee.  Thou art greater than I, and Thou canst only dwell in me by raising me to Thyself.  From the single fact that Thou dwellest in me, I of necessity must dwell in Thee.

**Practice:**  Dwell in God by thought and desire.

ಜಯ❀ಲಲ

### 221 ~ Wednesday

**"He that loveth Me not keepeth not My words."**
**~ St. John (14:24)**

**Thought:**  Do not deceive yourself, do not think that you can deceive God.  If your wishes are not according to the wishes of Jesus – if you do not the bidding of Jesus, you love Him not, you are not united with Him in heart and will.

**Prayer:**  Jesus, I love Thee, and I desire what Thou desirest; but I am weak, and without Thy assistance I shall not have strength to do Thy wishes, which indeed are my wishes too.

**Practice:** Fulfil the duties and rules of your state in life; obey your superiors, who in their respective positions represent Jesus Christ.

ಜ಼಼ಌ⊛ಌಌ

## 222 ~ Thursday

**"But the Paraclete, the Holy Ghost, whom the Father will send in My name, He will teach you all things." ~ St. John (14:26)**

**Thought:** The Holy Ghost is the Paraclete, or the Consoler, because He is the Light and the Flame. The Light, for He enlightens the understanding, and dissipates the error which laid it desolate. The Flame, for He warms and reanimates the heart when weakened.

**Prayer:** Jesus, inform me by the Holy Ghost of all those things that I should do for the glory of Thy Father.

**Practice:** Continual invocation of the Holy Ghost.

ಜ಼಼ಌ⊛ಌಌ

## 223 ~ Friday

"Peace I leave with you, My peace I give unto you." ~ St. John (14:27)

**Thought:**  Peace is the dying bequest of Jesus: peace of mind confirmed by faith in the word of Jesus; peace of heart strengthened by charity, which consists in obeying the instructions of Jesus Christ, and following the inspiration of the Holy Ghost.  Such is the order of things, peace is the tranquillity of order.

**Prayer:** Jesus, Thou alone canst give me peace. The world gives only disorder, and consequently tumult and anxiety.  Without Thee I can neither obtain nor persevere in that tranquillity of disposition which constitutes peace.

**Practice:**  Seek peace, but only through Jesus Christ.

ಞಞ☸ಞಞ

## 224 ~ Saturday

"But that the world may know that I love the Father; and as the Father has given Me commandment, so do I.  Arise, and let us go hence." ~ St. John (14:31)

**Thought:** Love does not show itself by sentiment or by words, but by *action*.  Do the bidding of Him you love, then will it be known that you love Him.  Jesus often repeats in the Gospel this doctrine already made so evident.  Let us not tire of meditating upon it, and repeating it to ourselves.

**Prayer:** Jesus, grant that I may go hence with Thee, and quickly and generously resolve to do what Thou and Thy Divine Father will.

**Practice:**  Prompt and entire fulfilment of the will of God.

ಬಙ ✲ ಲಗಬಙ ✲ ಲಗಬಙ ✲ ಲಗ

## 225 ~ Trinity Sunday
## First Sunday After Pentecost

**"In the name of the Father and of the Son and of the Holy Ghost." ~ St. Matthew (28:19)**

**Thought:**  Created to the image and likeness of God, baptised in the name of the Father, and of the Son, and of the Holy Ghost, I am called to live for ever in the company of the Three Persons of the august Trinity, and to share their happiness and glory.  How can I forget the dignity of my condition and destiny?

**Prayer:** O Father, Thou didst create me, I consecrate to Thee my mind and all my thoughts.  O Son, Thou didst redeem me, I consecrate to Thee my memory and my whole speech.  Holy Ghost, Thou didst sanctify me, I consecrate to Thee my will and all my affections.

**Practice:** Do all your actions in the name of the Father and of the Son and of the Holy Ghost.

**"Show us the Father, and it is enough for us."**
**~ St. John (14:8)**

**Thought:** God the Father is the beginning of the Son and Holy Ghost, the beginning of all that is and all that can be. He who sees the beginning sees all, for everything depends upon the beginning. Therefore to see the Father is to see both the Word, which is the wisdom of the Father, and the Holy Ghost, which is the goodness of the Father and the Son. In the Father we see the reason for all existing things; and to see the Father is supreme, complete happiness of the *mind*, and consequently of the will.

**Prayer:** Jesus, show us the Father: reveal Him to us here below by faith, and in heaven above by the light of glory.

**Practice:** Aspire towards God alone.

ಜಿಜಿ ✤ ೧೨೦೩

## 227 ~ Tuesday

**"And the Word was made flesh."**
**~ St. John (1:14)**

**Thought:** The Word has become like to me, that I may become like to Him, not God, but son of God; not son of God by nature, but by adoption; so shall I partake of the glorious happy life of the Divine nature.

**Prayer:** Jesus, Word, made flesh, true God, and true Son of God and of Mary, obtain for me from thy Father and grant me from Thyself the grace of resembling Thee and Thy word, of representing Thee in my life, of speaking of Thee continually in my discourse, just as Thou art the representative, the splendour of the glory of Thy Father, the word, the echo, and the wisdom of supreme understanding.

**Practice:** Imitate Jesus in your thoughts, words, and actions.

ಐ೫೦✿ಲೞೞ

## 228 ~ Wednesday

**"Thou shalt send forth Thy Spirit, and they shall be created; and Thou shalt renew the face of the earth." ~ Psalm 103 (30)**

**Thought:** Vainly the Father creates me, vainly the Son redeems me, if the Holy Ghost comes not down to me I am chaos – a body without life. It is by the working of the Holy Ghost that this chaos becomes a world, that this body receives life, that this soul lives by grace, and that the death of sin gives place to supernatural life.

**Prayer:** Jesus, send forth unto me Thy Spirit, the Spirit of Thy Father, which will enlighten my understanding and strengthen my will. Without It I am incapable of a single good thought, of one good desire.

**Practice:** Invoke the Holy Ghost at the commencement of your principal actions.

༺ఙ೩❀ಌಊ༻

## 229 ~ Thursday - Corpus Christi

**"For My Flesh is meat indeed, and My Blood is drink indeed." ~ St. John (6:56)**

**Thought:** The Body and Blood of Jesus Christ are inseparable from His Divinity. This Flesh then is Divine nourishment, and this Blood is Divine drink. But this nourishment, this drink, is not transformed into our substance to live by our life but it transforms us into its substance, that we may live by the Divine life of Jesus Christ.

**Prayer:** Jesus, be Thou my life – life of my mind, for Thou art truth and wisdom – life of my will, for Thou art all love and goodness.

**Practice:** Unite your intentions to those of the Heart of Jesus, that you may keep in you the Divine Life which you have received by Holy Communion.

༺ఙ೩❀ಌಊ༻

## 230 ~ Friday

**"He that eateth My Flesh, and drinketh My Blood, abideth in Me, and I in him."**
**~ St John (6:57)**

**Thought:** As the soul is in the body and the body is in the soul, and as the soul keeps and really maintains the body more than the body does the soul, so after Communion I am in Jesus, and Jesus is in me; He sustains and reanimates me, restores new life within me, deifies me[6], preserving in me at the same time my natural life and power.

**Prayer:** Jesus, dwell in me, and permit me to be Thy agent as my body is the agent of my soul; grant that all my actions may be performed for Thee, that I may live only in Thee.

**Practice:** Be guided and governed by Jesus.

ಬಿಜಿ❀ಚಿಲಿ

### 231 ~ Saturday

**"As the living Father hath sent Me, and I live by the Father; so he that eateth Me, the same also shall live by Me." ~ St. John (6:58)**

**Thought:** As the Word, Christ Jesus lives the life of the Father; as man He lives the human life, and also the Divine Life, which as the Word He received from His Father, and which He Himself communicates to His humanity. Nourished in Holy Communion by the Body and the Blood, by the Soul and the Divinity of Jesus, I shall live both in His human and Divine life.

---

6   An older expression meaning to be one with God through union with Him, not that we pray to become a 'deity'.

221

**Prayer:** Jesus, give me life from Thy life, thought from Thy thoughts, desires from Thy desires, love from Thy love, suffering and actions from Thy suffering and actions.

**Practice:** Spend your life in conformity with the life of Jesus.

ಖಖ⊛ಌಜಖಖ⊛ಌಜಖಖ⊛ಌಜ

## 232 ~ Second Sunday After Pentecost

**"This is the Bread that came down from heaven." ~ St. John (6:59)**

**Thought:** The Word made Flesh is the Bread, the nourishment of the soul – Bread of the intelligence, for it is Truth – savoury Bread, for it is wisdom – Bread of the will, for it is the Life, the origin of every movement, of every energy and virtue.

**Prayer**: Jesus, Thou art the Light, the Wisdom, the Virtue from on high – Thou art the Life! If I follow Thee not, I wander from Thee. Thou art Truth; if I believe Thee not, I deceive myself. Thou art the Life; if I am not united to Thee, then I die.

**Practice:** Every day I eat material food, so every day should I partake of Heavenly Food by Holy Communion, or at least by Spiritual Communion.

ಖಖ⊛ಌಜ

222

**"Not as your fathers did eat manna, and are dead." ~ St. John (6:59)**

**Thought:** And yet this manna was sent from heaven – a gift of God, but not God Himself. The purest and most heavenly of divine gifts are unable to satisfy the soul; God alone can stay that hunger, that thirst after infinite, eternal good which torments us. God alone is the life of the intellect and the will.

**Prayer:** Jesus, all that is not like to Thee is like to the dewdrop, which a ray of sunlight destroys. Thou alone canst satisfy me.

**Practice:** Do not be contented when you receive consolation; seek repose in Jesus, and in Jesus only.

ಟುಕ್ಟಿ ✠ ಲ್ಟುಟ್ಟ

**234 ~ Tuesday**

**"He that eateth this Bread shall live forever."
~ St. John (6:59)**

**Thought:** The life of man consists in the perfect union of the soul both with God and the body. There is some power which the soul may not exercise without the body. The intelligence and the will are not satisfied without a full knowledge and love of God. Eternal life is the irrevocable, indissoluble union of the soul with God and the body. Jesus guarantees us this eternal and complete life by Holy Communion.

**Prayer:** Jesus, Thou art the Bread of Life, the Life of the mind, for Thou art the Word – the Word of Truth; Life of the will, for Thou art the splendour of the glory of the Father the reflection of Divine Beauty; the Life of the senses and the body, for Thou art the Resurrection.

**Practice:** Often unite your actions to those of Jesus.

ಜಯ⊛ಇಲ

## 235 ~ Wednesday

### "Take ye and eat." ~ 1 Cor. (2:24)

**Thought**: Jesus commences the mystery of His union with us, and will accomplish it; but we must respond to His call by making at least an effort to take and receive the Divine Food which He offers – *Accipte*, Take ye, *et manducate*, and eat.

**Prayer:** Jesus, teach me to reply to Thy invitation by an ardent desire to receive Thee, and to become united to Thee.

**Practice:** Think of your past Communion, and look forward to the future Communion.

ಜಯ⊛ಇಲ

## 236 ~ Thursday

**"This is My Body; ... this chalice is the New Testament in My Blood."**
**~ 1 Cor. (11:24-25)**

**Thought:** Under the appearance of bread I receive and partake of the Body of Jesus; under the appearance of wine I receive and drink the Blood of Jesus. United with Jesus, and transformed into Him, my life will be like that of Jesus, a Christian and divine life.

**Prayer:** Thou art mine, and I am Thine. Live Thou in me, that I may dwell in Thee.

**Practice:** Let us incessantly remember how great is the dignity to which we are raised by Holy Communion.

ಜಞ⊕ಅಅ

## 237 ~ Friday
## Feast of the Sacred Heart

**"One of the soldiers with a spear opened His side." ~ St. John (19:34)**

**Thought**: Behold now that Heart which has loved mankind so dearly, and received only indifference or outrage in return! And yet, what does this Heart ask in exchange? My heart – nothing more, but nothing less.

**Prayer:** Jesus; I give Thee my heart – that is, my will, my liberty, my love, my strength; and it is to my interest to do this, for all that is not consecrated to Thee is lost for all eternity.

**Practice:** Unite all your intentions to those of Jesus Christ.

ಐಐ❀ଉଉ

### 238 ~ Saturday

**"Put me as a seal upon thy heart, as a seal upon thy arm." ~ Cant. (8:6)**

**Thought:** Wax takes the impression of the seal; so shall my heart take the impression of the Heart of Jesus. His wishes shall be my wishes. His Love shall by my love. Thus shall my arm receive from the Heart of Jesus strength, movement, action, being; and thus fortified my actions shall agree with those of Jesus.

**Prayer:** Jesus, by Thy Heart be Thou the centre, the mover of all my actions and affections.

**Practice:** Think as Jesus thinks, desire what Jesus desires, do as Jesus does.

ಐಐ❀ଉଉ

## 239 ~ Third Sunday After Pentecost

"Now the publicans and sinners drew near unto Him to hear Him." ~ St. Luke 15

**Thought:**  The world looks down upon the publicans, Jesus does not repel them.  Heaven rejects sinners, Jesus allows them to approach Him.  Whilst there remains in the soul any degree, however small, of good-will, there is still hope for its salvation.  O you who are despised by the world and rejected by heaven, draw near to Jesus!  Hear Him; there are words of pardon for you in the Heart of Jesus.

**Prayer:** Jesus, Thou art night and day upon the altar awaiting my visit, ready to grant all my requests, all my prayers.  Speak, O Jesus!  Tell me Thy desires; Thy servant listens.

**Practice:** Follow with docility the inspirations of Jesus.

ಜಾಜಾ ✿ ಚಿಚ3

## 240 ~ Monday

"And the Pharisees and the Scribes murmured, saying, This man receiveth sinners, and eateth with them." ~ St. Luke (15:2)

**Thought:** Jesus, who is Wisdom and Goodness itself, escapes not the criticism of those who in the eyes of the world are deemed master of wisdom and models of virtue, such as the doctors of the law and the Pharisees. Let us remember that the disciple is not above the Master.

**Prayer:** Jesus, grant that following Thy example I may count as nothing the murmur and criticisms of the world.

**Practice:** Do good, and let the world have its say.

෩෩✿෨෨

## 241 ~ Tuesday

"Rejoice with me, because I have found the sheep that was lost." ~ St. Luke (15:6)

**Thought:** The Good Shepherd loves all His sheep. Those in the fold run no danger, therefore they do not excite solicitude and anxiety. It is different with that sheep which has strayed from the flock; she is lost unless the Shepherd find her again. The joy in finding makes up for the pain caused by the anxiety of the search.

**Prayer:** Jesus, I lose myself at every instant by following my thoughts and my caprices when I should follow and imitate Thee. Where should I be this day hadst Thou not sought me out whenever I was lost.

**Practice:** Contrition and confidence.

ಬಾಶಾ ✪ ಞಲಞ

## 242 ~ Wednesday

**"I say to you, that even so there shall be joy in heaven upon one sinner that doth penance more than upon ninety-nine just who need not penance."** ~ St. Luke (15:7)

**Thought:** And why? Because the repentant sinner is often more humble, more grateful, more fervent than the just man who has never sinned; because the sinner's conversion costs God more than the perseverance of the just. More of grace is required to draw the wicked away from sin than to maintain the just in the path of virtue. Even if the grace were the same, the good result would be greater. A gift of a hundred pounds is a greater gift for a poor man than for a rich man.

**Prayer:** Jesus, help me to atone by fervour for the faults of my past life.

**Practice:** Work for the conversion of sinners.

ಬಾಶಾ ✪ ಞಲಞ

## 243 ~ Thursday

**"Or what woman having ten groats, if she should lose one groat, doth not light a candle."**
**~ St. John (15:8)**

**Thought:** When we lose some grace, we should light our lamp and examine out conscience to discover the cause of this infidelity.

**Prayer:** Jesus, teach me to value the least of Thy favours, and never to lose even one of those groats which Thou hast confided to me.

**Practice:** Continual watchfulness and care.

ಜುಜ೦ ⊕ ಲ೨೦ಜ

## 244 ~ Friday

**"She (doth) sweep the house." ~ St. Luke (15:8)**

**Thought:** Would you recover lost grace and fervour in God's service? Then examine your conscience, purify it of its smallest faults, sweep out the dust that prevents you from seeing; destroy those cobwebs, those vicious affections which harass the liberty of your heart.

**Prayer:** Jesus, seek me Thyself when I wander from Thee and am lost. I shall never recover Thee and return to Thee without Thy aid.

**Practice:** Make a faithful examination of conscience.

಼ಉಜಿ✽ಚಿ

## 245 ~ Saturday

**"And (doth) seek diligently until she find it."**
**~ St. Luke (15:8)**

**Thought:** You lose some precious object, say a piece of money, and you give yourself no rest until it is recovered. You lose the grace of God by mortal sin, or you lose some portion of that Divine gift by venial sin; do you regret this loss? Do you hasten to repair the loss?

**Prayer:** Jesus, help me to recover by my diligence the numberless graces I have lost during my lifetime.

**Practice:** Do all things well, such is the secret. Firstly, never lose a single instant; secondly, make up for lost time.

಼ಉಜಿ✽ಚಿ

ಜಞ❀ಆಚಣಞ❀ಆಚಣಞ❀ಆಚ

## 246 ~ Fourth Sunday After Pentecost

**"When the multitude pressed upon Him to hear the word of God, He stood by the Lake of Genesareth," ~ St. Luke (5:1)**

**Thought:** Do you desire popularity?  Then preach of God.  God alone interests all men, and especially the crowd, which is mostly composed of the unfortunate.  Popularity acquired by flattering the passions is of a different sort, fatal both to the people and to him who has recourse to it.  We do not save our souls by damning the soul of our neighbour.

**Prayer**: Jesus, Thou seekest the people, not popularity. *Et ipse stabat.* Thou dost not stoop to beg the favour of the public.  No; Thou standest up – *stabat.* Fill me with the like calmness and firmness.

**Practice:** Be calm in the midst of the world.

ಜಞ❀ಆಚ

## 247 ~ Monday

**"And going up into one of the ships that was Simon's, He desired him to draw back a little from the land; and sitting, He taught the multitudes out of the ship." ~ St. Luke (5:3)**

**Thought:** Jesus seats Himself and takes possession of Simon's ship. So shall He one day seat Himself in the religious society of which Peter shall be the head, and there preach to the people, (the Church). He desires that the ship be drawn back a little from the land. The Church should be some distance from the earth – i.e., separated from the material and temporal interests. Let the distance be not too great, lest Jesus be not heard. Man lives upon the earth, and is busied with earthly concern; the Church without setting value on such things must understand what man is permitted, nay, even commanded to do for the cares and sustenance of daily life.

**Prayer:** Jesus, may I never be separated from St. Peter, for whilst with him I shall also be with Thee.

**Practice:** Docility to the doctrine of the Church.

𝕭𝖀𝖘❀𝖈𝖆𝕺𝕾

## 248 ~ Tuesday

**"Launch out into the deep, and let down your nets for a draught."** ~ St. Luke (5:4)

**Thought:** With Jesus we may risk our lives upon the deep. There is nothing to be feared; success is certain. Let us advance, but under conduct of our Leader. To Peter only does Jesus say, *duc* – command – lead the way; to all the rest, *laxate retia*, cast your nets. They are to work and help Peter.

**Prayer:** Jesus, inspire me with some bold generous thought, and teach me to participate in Thy glory by the salvation of souls.

**Practice:** Let us try to take and save those souls which lose themselves in the sea of this world.

సంఘ❀శుభ

### 249 ~ Wednesday

**"We have laboured all night, and have taken nothing; but at Thy word I will let down the net." ~ St. Luke (5:5)**

**Thought:** When I labour without Jesus I labour in the dark; when I labour with Jesus I labour in the light. When I work with a human motive, my labour is unsuccessful; when it is by the order of Jesus, success is certain.

**Practice:** Offer up your intentions at the beginning of each action.

**Prayer:** Jesus, I will undertake nothing without Thee or without Thy order.

సంఘ❀శుభ

234

## 250 ~ Thursday

**"They enclosed a very great number of fishes." ~St. Luke (5:6)**

**Thought:** Obedience and faith are the two things necessary for success. But inspiration of faith and orders of obedience must be merited by perseverance in a hard and, what at times may appear, useless labour. We can do nothing without grace. But God will not grant us this grace until by the failure of our efforts we are convinced of our weakness.

**Prayer:** Jesus, when wilt Thou address to me that word which rewards effort and assures success?

**Practice:** Refer the results of your labour to God alone.

## 251 ~ Friday

**"Depart from me, for I am a sinful man, O Lord." ~ St. Luke (5:8)**

**Thought:** At the sight of this miraculous draught Simon, recognising the Divinity of Jesus, considers himself unworthy to remain any longer in His presence. Success in our labours, far from exalting us, should fill us with a sense of our own unworthiness.

**Prayer:** Jesus, come to me, dwell in me solely because I am a sinner, and because without Thee I can do nothing for Thy glory, for the salvation of souls, or for my own salvation.

**Practice:** Do not attribute to yourself the success of your own efforts.

ಬಌ✸ಚಚ

## <u>252 ~ Saturday</u>

**"Fear not; from henceforth thou shalt catch men."** ~ St. Luke (5:10)

**Thought:** Respond with fidelity to the first grace sent you by God. Refer all the glory of your success to Him. This first success, this first favour will be as nothing to the gifts and fruits which will reward your fidelity and humility. So the miraculous draught with which Peter was rewarded was but a symbol of the draught far more miraculous which he was to make by one single sermon when he converted three thousand persons to Jesus Christ.

**Prayer:** Jesus, grant me grace to deserve by my faithfulness in little things the glory of converting many souls to Thee.

**Practice:** Labour and pray for the salvation of souls.

ಬಌ✸ಚಚ

༺ꠁ❀ꠁꠂꠁꠁ❀ꠁꠂꠁꠁ❀ꠁꠂ

## 253 ~ Fifth Sunday After Pentecost

**"Unless your justice abounds more than that of the Scribes and Pharisees, you shall not enter into the kingdom of heaven."**
**~ St. Matthew (5:20)**

**Thought:** Why so? Because the perfection of these men was only on the surface – mere hypocrisy and vanity. Pagans even have allowed that the truly just man is not satisfied with merely appearing just.

**Prayer:** Jesus, help me to despise human judgement, teach me to do nothing on account of the esteem or the contempt of man.

**Practice:** Have Jesus ever before you.

༺ꠁ❀ꠁꠂ

## 254 ~ Monday

**"You have heard that it was said to them of old."** ~ St. Matthew (5:21)

**Thought:** Jesus repeats the law of Moses, and after restoring to it its former perfection He raises it still higher. God works on the same plan, ever improving His work. Constancy and progress! Advance, but advance always in the same direction, otherwise your progress will be useless.

237

**Prayer:** Jesus, give me firmness to adhere to the resolutions which Thou inspirest me with; so that being docile to Thy new inspiration I may always walk in the same path.

**Practice:** Firmness of resolution.

ಬಙ☸ಚಚ

## 255 ~ Tuesday

**"Thou shalt not kill ... Whosoever shall kill shall be in danger of the judgement."**
**~ St. Matthew (5:21)**

**Thought:** If it be a sin to take the life of the body, what a crime it must be to deprive the soul of life and eternal happiness by the scandal of word or of example. We should never forgive ourselves were we to cause death to a fellow-creature by an act of imprudence. How many words fall from our lips, how many actions do we not perform, which have more fatal effect upon souls than any imprudence could have upon the body!

**Prayer:** Jesus, grant that I may never scandalise by my negligence or by my folly one of those for whom Thou didst die upon the Cross.

**Practice:**  Watch over your words and actions, watch over all things that might scandalise any person, especially the weak-minded ones.

ಖಜಾ❀ಞಲಚ

## 256 ~ Wednesday

**"But I say to you, that whosoever is angry with his brother shall be in danger of the judgement." ~ St. Matthew (5:22)**

**Thought:** Anger does not repair an offence committed; it hurts him who gives way to it much more that it hurts him whom it threatens, for it blinds and carries man away, depriving him of the use of reason and liberty, and changing the man into the brute.

**Prayer:** Jesus, meek and humble of heart, calm within me all sentiments opposed to charity; teach me to forgive and forget injuries.

**Practice:**  Guard against the first impulses of anger.

ಖಜಾ❀ಞಲಚ

## 257 ~ Thursday

**"And whosoever shall say to his brother, Racca, shall be in danger of the council."**
**~ St. Matthew (5:23)**

239

**Thought:** Anger which is displayed is generally more sinful than anger which is felt but not shown. It is already judged, and it only remains to inflict the punishment. Watch over your words, and never let one word escape you that is contrary to the charity and respect due to your brother.

**Prayer:** Jesus, grant me so great a command over my speech, that I may never wound my neighbour.

**Practice:** Be silent when you feel anger in your heart.

ജ്ഞ✿ഛ

### 258 ~ Friday

**"And whosoever shall say, Thou fool, shall be in danger of hell fire." ~ St. Matthew (5:22)**

**Thought:** God is severe towards the man who insults his fellow man, for man is the image of God. To 'insult' the image of God is to insult God in His image.

**Prayer:** Jesus, teach me to understand the dignity of man for whom Thou thoughtest fit to die.

**Practice:** Respect for your neighbour.

ജ്ഞ✿ഛ

## 259 ~ Saturday

## "Go first to be reconciled to thy brother."
## ~ St. Matthew (5:24)

**Thought:** If you love God, love His work - His *chef d´oeuvre* – His likeness. If you desire God's pardon, forgive your brother whose offences against you are incomparably lighter than are yours against God.

**Prayer:** Jesus, forgive me as I forgive, love me as I love – but give me the grace to forgive and to love as Thou hast forgiven and loved.

**Practice:** Forgive and forget injuries.

૨૭૦ ✤ ૭૭૭૩૭ ✤ ૭૭૭૩૭ ✤ ૭૭


## 260 ~ Sixth Sunday After Pentecost

## "There was a great multitude, and they had nothing to eat." ~ St. Mark (8:1)

**Thought:** When following Jesus everything is forgotten in thinking of Him. His Word so nourishes the soul that we think not of bodily nourishment. But Jesus forgets not those who forget themselves to follow Him.

**Prayer:** Jesus, I will hear Thee and Thee only. Thy word is truth. I will follow Thee only. Thy example is my road of life.

**Practice:** Forget all things for Jesus Christ.

ಚಿಖಿ❀ಣ೮ಚ

## 261 ~ Monday

**"Calling His disciples together He saith to them, I have compassion on the multitude."**
**~ St. Mark (8:1-2)**

**Thought:** We never lose anything by forgetting ourselves and by following Jesus. His Heart is an abyss of mercy and His compassion will not be sterile. See how He calls His apostles, how He tells them of His compassion and His solicitude for the unfortunate.

**Prayer:** Jesus, into Thy Heart I confide all my miseries, all my cares. I will also share Thy solicitude for the unfortunate, and especially for the multitude.

**Practice:** Confidence in the Heart of Jesus, charity towards the poor.

ಚಿಖಿ❀ಣ೮ಚ

## 262 ~ Tuesday

**"Behold they have now been with Me three days, and have nothing to eat."**
**~ St. Mark (8:2)**

**Thought:** Constancy is always rewarded. When even everything shall fail you, when you have no hope whatever, follow Jesus, continue to pray and listen to Him. He may seem to bring you there to die of hunger – but leave Him not – even if it require a miracle – He will do it to reward your constancy.

**Prayer:** Jesus, Thou art my only hope, my sole place of repose. Go where Thou wilt, I will follow Thee.

**Practice:** Confidence in Jesus.

ಬಞಞ✿ಞಞ

## 263 ~ Wednesday

**"From whence can any one fill them here with bread in the wilderness." ~ St. Mark (8:4)**

**Thought:** God is always at hand when our human weakness is proved and acknowledged. In order that we may succeed let us do everything in our power. God wishes it. We must remember, however, that although we must work, our work will be useless without the Divine help.

**Prayer:**   Jesus; I acknowledge that without Thee, I am incapable of nourishing those souls confided to me by Thee.

**Practice:** Mistrust self, confide in God.

ಬಜ಼⊕ಲ಼ಚ

## 264 ~ Thursday

**"How many loaves have ye?  Who said, seven."**
**~ St. Mark (8:5)**

**Thought:**   What are seven loaves to feed so many thousand men?  Of what use are your poor talents, your ordinary virtues for the salvation of souls? How can you by yourself, or even with several to help you, contend against multitudes of unbelievers? Granted you can do little; yet you can do *something*. Begin then to do that little, and God will do the rest, and by your hand and by your working He will multiply the little you have done.

**Prayer:**   Jesus, I give and confide to Thy Heart the little that I know and the little that I am able to do; with Thee, who out of nothing workest miracles, I shall know and do all things.

**Practice:** Do what you are able.

ಬಜ಼⊕ಲ಼ಚ

## 265 ~ Friday

**"And taking the seven loaves, ... He gave to His disciples for to set before them."**
**~ St. Mark (8:6)**

**Thought:** Jesus has no need of our help to feed the hungry or enlighten the ignorant; but wishful to associate us with His glory, He deigns to borrow our assistance. He reserves what seems impossible to Himself and asks of us what is easily performed, the impossible action is the multiplying of the loaves; nothing is more easy than to receive them from the hands of Jesus and serve them to the people.

**Prayer:** Jesus, when wilt Thou deign to employ me in Thy service and in that of my neighbour?

**Practice:** Respond faithfully to the inspiration of grace.

ॐ✿❀

## 266 ~ Saturday

**"And they did eat and were filled."**
**~ St. Mark (8:8)**

**Thought:** Happy are those who forget everything and follow Jesus. Jesus takes upon Himself to feed and satisfy them. Happy they who confide in the tender care of the Heart of Jesus. The desires of their heart shall be more than accomplished.

**Prayer:** Jesus, Thou dost keep me waiting for the graces which I ask of Thee; but Thou wilt grant them, I believe it, and I hope it. Thou wilt not only grant me all I desire, but more even than I dare to hope for.

**Practice:**   Renew your confidence in Jesus, by oft repeated acts.

ಉಕಾ ✸ ಚಿಡುಉಕಾ ✸ ಚಿಡುಉಕಾ ✸ ಚಿಡು

## 267 ~ Seventh Sunday After Pentecost

### "Beware of false prophets."
### ~ St. Matthew (7:15)

**Thought:** The false prophet is worse than the thief or the assassin. The malefactor, at least, does not declare evil to be good. It is possible to lead back to virtue the man who commits evil through passion. But that man who teaches evil, whose mind is as corrupted as his heart, can only be converted by a double miracle.

**Prayer:** Jesus, Thou hast been as severe towards false preachers as Thou hast been kind towards the sinner. Fill me with a holy hatred of error and falsehood.

**Practice:** Combat error with unflagging zeal.

ಉಕಾ ✸ ಚಿಡು

## 268 ~ Monday

**"Who come to you in the clothing of sheep."**
**~ St. Matthew (7:15)**

**Thought:** The wicked man does not show himself in his true colours. He is too hideous, he is too cunning. Error puts on the mask of truth, vice adopts a virtuous aspect. The wolf dresses himself in sheep's clothing and the simple are deceived.

**Prayer:** Jesus, give me the simplicity of the dove, but give me also the prudence of the serpent; simplicity to think ill of no one; prudence to mistrust and recognise the deceiver.

**Practice:** Judge no one either for good or evil without proof attesting good or evil.

ৰুঙ্গ ❀ ণ্ডেওও

## 269 ~ Tuesday

**"By their fruits you shall know them"**
**~ St. Matthew (6:16)**

**Thought:** As soon as a man professes to teach falsehood and evil, he is judged. He that habitually speaks against reason or faith is a sophist, an infidel, or a fool. A man should not be thought good simply because his words are good. Sometimes the seducer quotes fine maxims, the better to deceive. Wait until his words are proved by his actions – then judge him.

**Prayer:** Jesus, teach me to mistrust those who belie their words by their conduct.

**Practice:** Actions are better than words.

೫ಙ⊛ಐ೪ಚ

## 270 ~ Wednesday

### "Do men gather grapes of thorns?"
### ~ St. Matthew (7:16)

**Thought:** False prophets and sophists are like to thorns. Subtle and artful they penetrate into souls but only to prick like thorns. Uneasiness and remorse, such are the fruits of the words of these false, wicked men.

**Prayer:** Jesus, why may I not labour with Thee to extirpate sophism and impiety, which corrupt both the mind and the heart?

**Practice:** Combat against bad doctrine.

೫ಙ⊛ಐ೪ಚ

## 271 ~ Thursday

**"A good tree cannot bring forth evil fruit, neither can an evil tree bring forth good fruit."
~ St. Matthew (7:18)**

**Thought:** The good tree is typical of the soul grafted upon Jesus Christ, and living of His life, the soul whose sap is the grace of God. Works produced by the influence of Jesus Christ and of His Spirit, which is the Holy Ghost, are fruits of supernatural and eternal life. The evil tree represents the soul cut off from Jesus Christ by sin – living and acting under the influence of the evil spirit, or at least living by the sole virtue of corrupted nature. How, then, can such works be good?

**Prayer:** Jesus, grant that I may live by Thy life, grant that all my actions may spring from Thee.

**Practice:** Unite your actions to those of Jesus.

ಜಞಐ❀ಞಐ

## 272 ~ Friday

**"Every tree that bringeth not forth good fruit shall be cut down, and shall be cast into the fire." ~ St. Matthew (7:19)**

**Thought:** What are good fruits? Fruit is the most useful and pleasing product of the tree. Nothing is useful and pleasing which does not draw us to God,

Who is the only true Good.  Every action that does not tend towards God is useless and only worthy to be cast into the fire, i.e., the fire of purgatory if venial sin, the fire of hell if mortal sin.

**Prayer:** Jesus, grant that by Thy help everything in me may tend towards Thy Father.

**Practice:** Let your intentions be pure and upright in everything.

ಬಿಎಂ✠ಲೞಲ

## 273 ~ Saturday

**"Wherefore by their fruits you shall know them." ~ St. Matthew (7:20)**

**Thought:**  Our action should correspond with our sentiments.  Faith without good works is a dead faith, faith without charity is a deformed faith.  Charity is essentially active.  Do not say that you love God and your neighbour unless you really desire the glory of God and the good of your neighbour.

**Prayer:** Jesus, give me the strength, and procure me the opportunity to prove to Thee my faith and my love be works and by fruits.

**Practice:** Let no day pass without doing some good work.

ಬಞ✸ಞಚಿಬಞ✸ಞಚಿಬಞ✸ಞಚಿ

## 274 ~ Eighth Sunday After Pentecost

**"There was a certain rich man who had a steward." ~ St. Luke (16:1)**

**Thought:** This rich man is God – I am the steward. I have received a soul, a body, and my share of the world, in fact, all that I might expect from Him, and I must render Him an account. To God I must render the account and the product of all my knowledge, possessions, power and actions.

**Prayer:** Jesus, in Thy Sacred Heart I place my thoughts, words, and actions. Take everything, and offer Thou me to Thy Heavenly Father.

**Practice:** Refer all you actions to the glory and service of God.

ಬಞ✸ಞಚಿ

## 275 ~ Monday

**"And the same was accused unto him, that he had wasted his goods." ~ St. Luke (16:1)**

**Thought:** I have wasted the goods confided to me by God. Who can calculate the losses occasioned by one sin? One single mortal sin is sufficient to deprive me of Heaven and God. One single venial sin, however, slight, suffices to deprive me of a degree of grace equivalent to a degree of eternal glory.

**Prayer:** Jesus, how long will my negligence and selfishness rob Thee of the glory Thou hast a right to expect from each of my actions?

**Practice:** Do all things well, for the glory of God.

ಐಐ✾ಐಐ

## 276 ~ Tuesday

### "Give an account of they stewardship."
### ~ St. Luke (16:2)

**Thought:** What account, O God, can I give Thee? What have I done for Thy glory? What have I done for my own sanctification? Thinking only of self, loving only self, I have not even understood my own interests, or if I did understand them I have not acted accordingly.

**Prayer:** Jesus, teach me each day to render both to myself and to Thee an exact account of my faithfulness in Thy service.

**Practice:** Examine your conscience daily.

ಐಐ✾ಐಐ

## 277 ~ Wednesday

**"For now thou canst be steward no longer."**
**~ St. Luke (16:2)**

**Thought:** Why does God allow you to be taken away from a certain position where you could labour for His glory and the salvation of souls? Because by your negligence you have not made good use of the situation, or because through your vanity you have made use of it solely for your own personal satisfaction; God then withdraws from you His confidence and the care of His affairs – *Jam non poteris villicare.*

**Prayer:** Jesus, cast me not altogether aside, permit me to strive a little longer for Thy glory and in Thy service.

**Practice:** When there is question of serving God, lose not one moment, not one opportunity.

ಊಕಾ✸ಚಾಚ್ಚ

## 278 ~ Thursday

**"For the children of this world are wiser in their generation than the children of light."**
**~ St. Luke (16:8)**

**Thought:** The children of this century unite to deceive and to destroy; the children of light either remain indifferent in the face of impiety, or, instead of helping one another and uniting against the enemy, are

253

divided and are fighting amongst themselves. The children of the world are for ever fettering the children of light by every means in their power: the children of light allow the children of the world to spread error and scandal.

**Prayer:** Jesus, endow Thy servants with energy and prudence – prudence to mistrust Thy enemies, energy to combat them.

**Practice:** Display the same activity for truth, for good, for the Church, as the wicked display for falsehood, for evil and for hell.

ಜಲಜಾ ✿ ಲ೩ಬ

## 279 ~ Friday

**"Make unto you friends of the mammon of iniquity."** ~ St. Luke (16:9)

**Thought:** Worldly goods have no value unless they are employed for the glory of God and the salvation of souls. Health, strength, talent, virtue, grace, all these gifts which we receive should be used for the good of man; and this good consists of union with God through a knowledge and love of Him.

**Prayer:** Jesus, teach me that heaven is the lot of those who are devoted to the service of their neighbour, and that eternal fire awaits the selfish who like the bad rich man are only busied with themselves.

**Practice:** When a day passes in which you have rendered no service to your neighbour, say with Titus, "I have lost a day."

ಜಲಜ⊛ಚಿಲಚ

## 280 ~ Saturday

**"He that is faithful in that which is least, is faithful in that which is greater."**
**~ St. Luke (16:10)**

**Thought:** It is easy then to become holy. For in little things I cannot excuse myself on account of my weakness. I cannot pass the whole day in prayer, but I may pray carefully for one quarter of an hour. I cannot imitate the austerities of a Saint Anthony, but I may abstain from some little sensuality, some useless word. I have it not in my power to travel through the East like St. Francis Xavier, but I can speak a kind word to this friend, to that poor person, to that sick man. Thus by these small easy actions I shall become capable of heroic actions.

**Prayer:** Jesus, nothing is little in Thy service, nothing is little when Thou dost desire it.

**Practice:** Perform a good work, make a little sacrifice or say a kind word at least once a day.

ಜಲಜ⊛ಚಿಲಚ

ರ⚜ ಲ⚜ರ⚜ಲ

## 281 ~ Ninth Sunday After Pentecost

**"If thou hadst known, and that in this thy day, the things that are to thy peace."**
**~ St. Luke (19:42)**

**Thought:** Jesus desires our happiness. Why do we resist His desires? Let Him establish His reign in our hearts. As a reward for the little services He asks of us, He will fill our soul with abundance of peace and consolation.

**Prayer:** Jesus, enter into my heart: reign there: dispose of it according to Thy own good pleasure. I know Thou only desirest my welfare.

**Practice:** Faithfully obey inspirations from above.

ರ⚜ಲ

## 282 ~ Monday

**"But now they are hidden from thy eyes."**
**~ St. Luke (19:42)**

**Thought:** We often do not understand things because we have no desire to understand them. Jerusalem did not recognise the Saviour by His word or by His miracles because she closed her eyes to the Light. When God in His Providence shows us His designs, let us obey His will and accomplish it.

Experience will teach us that the Divine ways are the ways of mercy.

**Prayer:** Jesus, I rely entirely upon Thy wisdom and bounty for all that concerns me.

**Practice:** Blind confidence in Jesus.

ಜಲ಼೨೫ఴ

## 283 ~ Tuesday

## "Thy enemies shall cast a trench about thee." ~ St Luke (19:43)

**Thought:** The enemies of the soul are the flesh, the devil, and the world. The flesh surrounds the soul with sensuality, the world besieges it with human respect, the demon completes the work of these two by sin. The soul, once a slave to the senses no longer accepts the help of grace; if a slave to human respect, it dares not follow the call of reason; if a slave to sin, it loses everything in losing God.

**Prayer:** Jesus! The example of Jerusalem teaches me that the soul which does not acknowledge Thy Royalty becomes the slave and prey of her enemies.

**Practice:** Serve Jesus if you do not wish to serve the world and hell.

ಜಲ಼೨೫ఴ

## 284 ~ Wednesday

**"They shall not leave in Thee a stone upon a stone." ~ St. Luke (19:44)**

**Thought:** When sin enters the soul it leaves not a stone upon a stone. It destroys grace, it falsifies reason, it enslaves the will, it corrupts the senses. It robs the soul of its virtues one by one – first of charity, then of hope, and finally of faith. All moral virtues disappear – prudence, justice, strength, temperance. Nothing is seen in a soul ravaged by sin but chaos and disorderly ruin.

**Prayer:** Jesus! Be Thou Master in my soul, otherwise, if abandoned as prey to the passions it will fall into the power of the devil, it will become a living hell.

**Practice:** Keep guard over your heart, especially by examination of conscience.

## 285 ~ Thursday

**"And entering into the temple, He began to cast out them that sold therein."**
**~ St. Luke (19:45)**

**Thought:** Jesus does not tolerate in His temple those who sell animals destined to the sacrifice. Would

He, then, have within His Church those who propagate doctrines contrary to His Gospel condemned by His Vicar?

**Prayer:** Jesus, drive out from my soul all worldly-wise calculation, which would purchase the liberty of saying and doing good by granting to others the permission to say and do ill.

**Practice:** Have no consideration for those who profane the sanctity of the Church by their doctrine or by their conduct.

ಬಞ ✿ ೧ೞ

## 286 ~ Friday

### "My house is the house of prayer."
### ~ St. Luke (19:46)

**Thought:** My soul should be a house of prayer. All my thoughts, desires, and actions should tend to the service and glory of God. Whenever I refer my actions to any other than God my soul becomes a den of thieves.

**Prayer:** Jesus! I consecrate to Thee myself, my possessions, my power, my actions.

**Practice:** Offer up at different times your actions to God.

ಬಞ ✿ ೧ೞ

## 287 ~ Saturday

### "And He was teaching daily in the temple."
### ~ St. Luke (19:47)

**Thought:** Jesus teaches, but unsuccessfully. His word meets only with contradiction; it does but irritate the fury of His enemies, confirming them in their resolution to destroy Him. Jesus nevertheless continues. Let us never tire either of repeating truth or of combating error, even though we convert no one, even though we increase the vexation of our adversaries. We may perhaps succumb, but we shall fall martyrs to truth, and truth will triumph.

**Prayer:** Jesus, fill me with constancy, and let me not be abashed either by seeming failure or by manifest opposition.

**Practice:** Recommence each day whatever you have undertaken for the service of God, and never give way to discouragement.

ಖಖ෴ಇ෴ಖಖ෴ಇ෴ಖಖ෴ಇ෴

## 288 ~ Tenth Sunday After Pentecost

**"And to some who trusted in themselves as just, and despised others, He spoke also this parable."** ~ St. Luke (18:9)

**Thought:** The very fact of trusting in one's self and mistrusting others is an injustice firstly towards

God in Whom alone we should place our confidence; and secondly towards our neighbour whom we have no right to judge, much less to despise.

**Prayer:**   Jesus, enlighten me as to Thee, as to my neighbour, and as to myself: as to Thee that I may understand that without Thee I am nothing; as to myself that I may recognise my nothingness and my misery; as to my neighbour that I may open my eyes to his merits and close them to his faults.

**Practice:**   Mistrust of self, and esteem for others.

ಬಙ⊕ಲಚ

## 289 ~ Monday

### "Two men went up into the temple to pray."
### ~ St. Luke (18:10)

**Thought:**   Of these two men, the one believes himself to be just, which he is not; the other believes himself a sinner, which he is.  The former is in error and pride strengthens him in it.  The latter is in the right, and his humility will draw him out of misery.

**Prayer:**   Jesus, I come to Thee with the knowledge and experience of my weakness and misery. My confidence in the past and in the future is in Thee, and in Thee alone.

**Practice:** Humility in prayer.

ಬಙ⊕ಲಚ

## 290 ~ Tuesday

**"The Pharisee standing, prayed thus with himself."** ~ St. Luke (18:11)

**Thought:** The proud man stands upright before God, and if he prays, he prays to himself; he cannot forget self. He thinks only of self, esteems only, loves only, self. Look at the worldly man of today; he stands upright "Phariseus stans." If there is any advantage it is in favour of the Pharisee of past ages. He did pray, though very badly. The worldly man of today never enters a church; why? No one knows. Not only does he not bend the knee before God, but rising up with haughty look and bearing, he talks, he is wearied, but he prays not.

**Prayer:** Jesus, I will bow the forehead before Thee, that I may not incline it before man.

**Practice:** Be humble before God, and you will be firm in the presence of man.

ಜಖ ⊛ ಞ೮ಙ

## 291 ~ Wednesday

**"O God, I give thee thanks that I am not as the rest of men."** ~ St. Luke (18:11)

**Thought:** Thus do I seem to hear the sophists of our times speak; those men so self-sufficient, so disdainful, so contemning, so convinced that they are the only wise, the only learned. The rest of mankind! What is it in the eyes of this proud being? Madman, were it as true as it is false that you are not an adulterer, an extortioner, an unjust man, know that you possess one vice which contains all the rest, that vice is called pride.

**Prayer:** Jesus, I confess and own that I am not as good as the rest of men, and that without Thee there is no crime which I might not commit.

**Practice:** Esteem yourself as the least among men.

ಬಿಜಿ⊛ಞಚಚ

## 292 ~ Thursday

**"And the publican standing afar off would not so much as lift up his eyes to heaven."**
**~ St. Luke (18:13)**

**Thought:** The publican also stands up, but far from the altar, for he considers himself unworthy to approach; nor does he dare to lift up his eyes towards that heaven which seems closed to him. Doubtless he is a sinner, but a humble, a repentant sinner. If he stands up, it is to show that he is ready to do all that God shall ask of him.

**Prayer:** Jesus, fill me with humble repentance for my faults, give me consciousness of my indignity, and knowledge of my misery.

**Practice:** Never forget what you are.

ಬಿಹಾ⊕ಡುಡಿ

## 293 ~ Friday

**"This man went into his house justified."**
**~ St. Luke (18:14)**

**Thought:** Everything is forgiven him that asks forgiveness – nothing is forgiven him that does not ask for it.  By asking for forgiveness we acknowledge our wrong and repent our fault.  By our silence, we do not own, but persist in the wrong.  The repentant sinner regains grace and justice, the proud Pharisee returns to his house as proud and as guilty as when he went out.

**Prayer:** Jesus, I repent; grant me that forgiveness which Thou didst obtain for me upon the cross, at the price of Thy Blood.

**Practice:** Humility and confidence.

ಬಿಹಾ⊕ಡುಡಿ

## 294 ~ Saturday

**"Every one that exalteth himself shall be humbled; he that humbleth himself shall be exalted." ~ St. Luke (18:14)**

**Thought:** God deals favourably with the meek of heart, but rejects the proud: mankind follows the same rule; therefore it is folly to exalt one's self. God and mankind exalt those who humble themselves. We should then humble ourselves with sincerity, for otherwise our hypocrisy would soon be discovered.

**Prayer:** Jesus, grant me a knowledge of myself and of Thee. Humility will then come easy to me. The knowledge of my misery will keep me in my place, the knowledge of Thy greatness will keep me at that distance which respects demands.

**Practice:** Never seek the highest place, take rather the lowest.

ಬ಄ ✸ ಲ಄ಬ಄ ✸ ಲ಄ಬ಄ ✸ ಲ಄

## 295 ~ Eleventh Sunday After Pentecost

### "And they bring him one deaf and dumb."
### ~ St Mark (7:32)

**Thought**: I am deaf to the inspirations of grace, and I am dumb when it behoves me to defend the interests of the Church. Who will teach me to be docile and faithful to the Divine Word? Who will give me courage to speak boldly in defence of faith and Church against the enemies of religion.

**Prayer:** Jesus, Thou alone canst work this wonder, Thou alone canst give me both courage and docility.

**Practice:** Hear the voice of God, and profess your faith without any human respect.

ಖಙ⚜ೕೞ

## 296 ~ Monday

**"And, taking him from the multitude apart, He put his fingers into his ears, and spitting, He touched his tongue."**
**~ St. Mark (7:33)**

**Thought:** Are you desirous of hearing the Word of God and learning the truth? If so, you must separate yourself from the crowd. In the midst of the world you can only hear the buzz of opinion. Noise is confusing, opinion is doubtful, and is oftentimes an echo of error. Do you wish for liberty of speech? You must still withdraw from the crowd. Surrounded by it, you would not dare to proclaim your thought. You, like the rest of the world, would speak under the control of your passions.

**Prayer:** Jesus, take me apart; if not, the crowd will drag me away; open my ears that I may listen to Thy Word, touch my tongue with Thy Precious Blood in the Holy Communion, that I may have knowledge and courage to speak of Thee.

**Practice:** Be docile to the calling of Jesus, do not heed the voice of the crowd.

ಖಙ⚜ೕೞ

## 297 ~ Tuesday

### "And looking up to heaven He groaned."
### ~ St. Mark (7:34)

**Thought:** Jesus looks up to heaven. Let us before the combat, by a pure and upright intention and by a humble yet confident invocation, look towards Him who can do all things, without Whom we can do nothing. Jesus groans. Human nature confesses its weakness. Let us confess our impotence, and we shall become powerful with the power of God.

**Prayer:** Jesus, by Thee, and through Thee only, do I expect strength and efficacy – strength to act, and success after action.

**Practice:** Cast one look towards God at the commencement of each action.

☙🌸❦

## 298 ~ Wednesday

### "And He said to him: Ephpheta, which is, Be thou opened." ~ St. Mark (7:34)

**Thought**: One word from Jesus suffices to open ear and mouth. When will this word be said for me? When shall I become docile to the voice of God? When shall I have grace to speak well of God?

**Prayer:** Jesus, say one word that I may hear and repeat it, both in my conduct and in my speech.

**Practice:** Expect everything from God alone.

ಚುಪು✤ಲಲಚ

## 299 ~ Thursday

**"And immediately his ears were opened, and the string of his tongue was loosed, and he spoke right." ~ St. Mark (7:35)**

**Thought:** He spoke right. He spoke correctly. *Loquebatur recte.* What is required in order to speak correctly, in the moral sense? Firstly, the ear of intelligence must be opened to the voice of grace; secondly, the chain of human respect binding the tongue must be broken. Then only will our language be correct – i.e., it will be in conformity with our thoughts and with reason because it will no longer be an echo of opinion, or the echo of the passions of man; it will be in conformity with the Divine thought and with faith, because the Word of God once listened to and received with docility will regulate our thoughts and words.

**Prayer:** Jesus, Eternal Wisdom, grant that my word may become a repetition of The Divine Word, that my wisdom may be Thy Wisdom.

**Practice:** Speak according to your belief and faith.

ಚುಪು✤ಲಲಚ

## 300 ~Friday

**"And He charged them that they should tell no man."** ~ St. Mark (7:36)

**Thought:** Jesus refuses worldly glory. Human judgement is so false! And we would do good, but on condition that the would should know it. What reward can man give to us? Let us raise up our hearts. Let us do good. God will judge and recompense us.

**Prayer:** Jesus, if Thou concealest Thy favours, it is not through fear of flattery, but through contempt for the vanity of human opinion.

**Practice:** Despise human judgement.


ಕುಶಿ❀ಞ೮ಶ

## 301 ~ Saturday

**"He hath done all things well."**
**~ St. Mark (7:37)**

**Thought:** Why has He done well? Because He has made the deaf to hear, the dumb to speak. How many are there now deaf to the voice of God! The greatest benefit that can be conferred on them is to teach them to hear the truth, by word and by book. How many are dumb in the service of the Lord, refusing to open their lips to defend Him! The best thing we can do is to loosen the strings of their tongues and obtain from them a frank, full, and complete declaration in favour of truth, justice, and the Church.

**Prayer:** Jesus, teach me to understand that all sanctity consists in doing good, and that doing good consists in serving our neighbour.

**Practice:** Do all things well. *Age quod agis.* Give yourself entirely up to the action you are performing.

ಖಙ❀ಲಚಙಖಙ❀ಲಚಙಖಙ❀ಲಚಙ

## 302 ~ Twelfth Sunday After Pentecost

**"Blessed are the eyes that see the things which you see." ~ St. Luke (10:23)**

**Thought:** Blessed are those who see Jesus, i.e. God made man, God made visible by the Incarnation. Wherefore should we envy those who saw Jesus during His mortal life? We see Him, we know Him to be present, living, working, teaching and speaking in His Church and through His Church which is His Body, and the evident, sensible manifestation of His Presence, His Wisdom, His Bounty, and His Power.

**Prayer:** Jesus, I see Thee by the eye of faith, by the eye of reason, and by the eye of the body. The eye of the body sees the Christian, the priest: the eye of the reason sees the action which distinguishes the Christian, the priest; the eye of faith recognises Thee in the Christian, and in the priest.

**Practice:** Recognise Jesus Christ in each member of His Church.

౮౿౸❀౸౿౺

## 303 ~ Monday

**"Master, what must I do to possess eternal life?"** ~ St. Luke (10:25)

**Thought:** According to the intention of the interrogator, this question is a test. So the question is admirably put, and the test is decisive. Any course of teaching which does not resolve this problem by precise and practical solution is imperfect, and give neither wisdom not science. Only that which has reference to eternal life is of service, all other is useless and a waste of time.

**Prayer:** Jesus, Thou alone hast the words of eternal life. Tell me what I must do to obtain this life. Give me strength to act according to Thy instructions.

**Practice:** Think only of eternal life.

౮౿౸❀౸౿౺

## 304 ~ Tuesday

**"What is written in the law."** ~ St. Luke (10:26)

**Thought:** Oftentimes we feign ignorance, not through humility but to avoid giving practical example.

271

That doctor who asks Jesus what the means are for gaining eternal life knows them very well, he is a doctor of the law, and the law contains all that is necessary for salvation.

**Prayer:** Jesus, enlighten me notwithstanding, and help me to acknowledge what I know already, and especially grant me strength to practice it.

**Practice:** Make use of the light already received if you wish to obtain more.

ಜಞ❀ಎ೧೮

### 305 ~ Wednesday

**"Thou shalt love the Lord thy God with thy whole heart, and with thy whole soul, and with all thy strength, and with all thy mind, and thy neighbour as thyself." ~ St. Luke (10:27)**

**Thought:** Such is the law. – *Diliges* – love of choice, free love – not blind love or instinctive love – *ex toto corde* – no affection which tends not towards God – *ex tota anima* – every constant instant of my life, every breath consecrated to God – *ex totis viribus* – all my strength, all the sinews of my body, all the tendencies of my soul directed to the service of God – *et ex omni mente* – all my thoughts and intentions tending towards God. All the reasons I have to love myself should equally impel me to love my neighbour. In myself I should love the work of God, the image of God, the child of God, the brother and member of Jesus Christ. My neighbour is all this.

**Prayer:** Jesus, I unite my intentions to those of Thy Divine Heart, and by so doing I am sure to accomplish the law.

**Practice:** Have effective as well as affective love.

ಬಐ✿ಞ೮೩

## 306 ~ Thursday

**"This do; and thou shalt live." ~St. Luke (10:28)**

**Thought:** It does not suffice to know our duty, we also *do* it. Oh! If we did all the good we know of and are able to do! To what perfection should we not arrive and how rapid would be our progress! Is it then so difficult to love God with all our strength? God asks for our whole strength, but for nothing more. We are not asked to do what is impossible. So with regard to our neighbour. We are asked to do for him what we do for ourself, not to do anything which is beyond our power.

**Prayer:** Jesus, enlighten, and strengthen me. Give me at least the good will to do what I know, and what I am able.

**Practice:** Let us not think of what we cannot do, but let us do what is in our power.

ಬಐ✿ಞ೮೩

**"Which of these three in thy opinion was neighbour to him that fell among robbers?"**
**~ St. Luke (10:36)**

**Thought:** Love is proved by actions. Your brother suffers. You pass him by without even looking at him. Say not that you love him. Your brother falls into the hands of the devil by sin, and it is in your power to enlighten him by good counsel and convert him. You make no attempt. You pass by as though the misfortunes of your neighbours concerned you not. You are wretched yourself. This cruel selfishness will cause your perdition, and in your turn you will fall into the hands of the devil.

**Prayer:** Jesus, grant that I may never be insensible to the temporal or spiritual misery of my neighbour.

**Practice:** Works of mercy.

ಜಿಙ್ಞ ❀ ಞಞಚ

**308 ~ Saturday**

**"Go and do thou I like manner."**
**~ St. Luke (10:37)**

**Thought:** The effects, the sign, and the proof of our love of God manifest themselves in the service we do our neighbour, in the consolation we afford him in time of suffering. Even the sinner, when doing works of charity, is efficaciously preparing himself to regain grace. You do not love God who is hidden from your sight unless you love and serve your brother, the child of God present to you. If, on the other hand, you love and serve your neighbour, you will soon love and serve your God.

**Prayer:** Jesus, Thou art the true Samaritan. Thou hast taken us, cured us of those wounds with which sin, after despoiling us, had loaded us. Grant that I may imitate Thee by my zeal for the salvation of my brethren.

**Practice:** Neglect no occasion of serving your neighbour.

ຮນຮາ ✧ ஜ౪ຮນຮາ ✧ ஜ౪ຮນຮາ ✧ ஜ౪

### 309 ~ Thirteenth Sunday After Pentecost

**"Going to Jerusalem Jesus passed through the midst of Samaria and Galilee."**
**~ St. Luke (17:11)**

**Thought:** Jerusalem represents the Church. Samaria is a type of schism, heresy, and rebellious Christians. Galilee, where paganism had been established during the captivity of Babylon, represents infidelity. In order to form and increase the Church, Jesus, by His Apostles and His missionaries, traverses the countries occupied by the pagans and bad Christians. The great work is the propagation of the faith and the conversion of degenerate Christians.

**Prayer:** Jesus, do not permit me to become useless here below. Grant that I may help in Thy work, which is the Church, by the conversion of sinners.

**Practice:** Work incessantly for the salvation of your neighbour.

৩৪৩❀৫৫৪

### 310 ~ Monday

**"There met Him ten men that were lepers, who stood afar off." ~ St. Luke (17:12)**

**Thought:** A certain passion, a certain fault, like leprosy, may appear incurable and incorrigible. Go to Jesus. Go to Him with confidence, humility, and constancy. With confidence – *occurrerunt ei* – present yourself; go meet Him with constancy – *steterunt* – stand before Him with determination to wait until your prayer is heard; with humility – *a longe* – consider how undeserving you are to approach Jesus.

**Prayer:** Jesus, Thou alone canst cure me. I will then stand before Thee, praying, until Thou shalt speak the word of salvation.

**Practice:** Be persevering in prayer.

৩৪৩❀৫৫৪

## 311 ~ Tuesday

**"And lifted up their voice, saying, Jesus, Master, have mercy on us." ~ St. Luke (17:13)**

**Thought:** Let us raise up our voices and persist the more the further we know ourselves to be from God. But I know not how to pray. What – you suffer – you are unhappy – and you know not how to pray? Acknowledge your misery, desire to break from it, turn towards Him alone who can help you – and you will have prayed.

**Prayer:** Jesus, have pity on me. Thou seest my misery far better than I – and Thou seest the remedy for the evil.

**Practice:** Simplicity and obstinacy in prayer.

ಐಐ✿ಐಐ

## 312 ~ Wednesday

**"Go show yourselves to the priests."
~ St. Luke (17:14)**

**Thought:** These lepers owe their cure to their obedience. First of all Jesus obeys the laws which constitute priests the judges of the cure of leprosy – then the lepers obeyed Jesus, and without waiting for their cure went unto the priest to state their complaint. They obeyed, and on the way they were cured.

Obedience and faith obtain the victory.

**Prayer:** Jesus, speak and I obey – speak and I believe. But add to Thy word the gift of grace, add impulse to inspiration. Without this, strength will fail me, and I shall not be able to follow the light.

**Practice:** Obey and believe.

ೞ๘๏๏

### 313 ~ Thursday

**"And it came to pass, as they went, they were made clean." ~ St. Luke (17:14)**

**Thought:** Pride engenders all vice. Obtain a cure for pride, and evil is destroyed in the roots. *Now*, obedience is precisely the antidote of pride. The lepers had scarcely entered on the path of obedience when they were cured.

**Prayer**: Jesus, distance does not exist with regard to Thee, or rather he is near to Thee who does what Thou commandest, even when the accomplishment of Thy orders seems to remove him from Thee. Minds are united more by the union of wills than by the proximity of bodies.

**Practice:** Confidence in the word of Jesus.

ೞ๘๏๏

## "Were not ten made clean, and where are the nine?" ~ St. Luke (17:17)

**Thought:**　In time of misfortune we pray, in time of happiness we forget to pray. Gratitude hangs heavily on us. Pride blushes to acknowledge that assistance has been required, indifference thinks not of remembering favours. Yet there is no injustice more deeply felt than ingratitude. Jesus who is so sweet, so humble, complains of this offence. Out of ten lepers one only is grateful and he is a Samaritan, one whom we would nowadays call a schismatic. Often those called good are ungrateful towards God, for they seem to think that favours are their due.

**Prayer:** Jesus, I mourn and am grieved at the ingratitude, the forgetfulness, the indifference shown to man. What can I say when I see the ingratitude to which Thou art subject?

**Practice:**　Show your gratitude towards God and towards those who are kind to you.

ಬಿಜ಼ ⊛ ಚ಼ಚಿ

## 315 ~ Saturday

**"Thy faith hath made thee whole."**
**~ St. Luke (17:19)**

**Thought:** Faith saves us, but not without good works. The Samaritan obtained salvation because impelled by faith he returned and threw himself at the feet of Jesus, thanking Him for his cure  But without faith, good works are worth nothing. Faith raises them and gives them supernatural efficaciousness.

**Prayer:** Jesus, in Thee alone will I confide, Thou art the only Saviour.

**Practice:** Spirit of faith in all your works.

ಜಞ❀ಞಚಜಞ❀ಚಜಜಞ❀ಚಜ

## 316 ~ Fourteenth Sunday After Pentecost

**"No man can serve two masters."**
**~ St. Matthew (6:24)**

**Thought:** Unless these masters are one and the same. Thus I can and must serve God the Father and Jesus His Son, and the Pope who is the Vicar of Christ, and my superiors (who each according to their degree) represent the One Master – i.e., God.  But it is impossible to serve two opposite masters, as God and the devil, Jesus Christ and Belial, the Church and the world, the spirit of the Gospel and the spirit of the times.

**Prayer:** Jesus, Thou alone art Master, I can, and will serve Thee alone.

**Practice:** Have God in sight through Jesus Christ and the Church.

ಜಜ⊛ಞಞ

## 317 ~ Monday

**"You cannot serve God and Mammon."**
**~ St. Matthew (6:24)**

**Thought:** To serve God is to raise one's self, to serve mammon is to lower one's self. We cannot mount and descend at the same time. What folly to balance between vile metal and Him Who is Eternal, Infinite Good. What degradation to value the soul less than the body, spiritual and eternal interest less than material and temporal interest. And yet this folly is the wisdom, the prudence of worldly man, and man glories in it!

**Prayer:** Jesus, give me to understand the first word of Thy preaching. Blessed are the poor in spirit and of heart. Break my chains, even if they are wrought of gold or silver.

**Practice:** Detach yourself from the riches of the world.

ಜಜ⊛ಞಞ

## 318 ~ Tuesday

"Be not solicitous for your life, what you shall eat, nor for your body, what you shall put on." ~ St. Matthew (6:25)

**Thought:**  Give yourself up to kind Providence, which will in due time procure for you what you require.  That which Jesus promises for the life of the body is still more true with regard to the wants of the soul.  Let us in all simplicity, and without solicitude, do our duty and our best.  God will do the rest.

**Practice:**  Have no useless anxious solicitude.

ಙಙ۞ಞಞ

## 319 ~ Wednesday

"Behold the birds of the air."
~ St. Matthew (6:26)

**Thought:**  The bird has no care.  It is always on the wing, seeking food in every place and always finding some.  So let us be active, always at work, but without solicitude.   Let us use our two wings, intelligence and will, to find nourishment for the soul, viz., truth and justice; but we must remember that without Providence all our efforts will be in vain, while on the contrary with the help of God our efforts will be crowned with success.  Let us not forget, however, that before helping us God expects that we should make good use of our reason and liberty.

**Prayer:** Jesus, I give up to Thee the direction of all my thoughts and desires.

**Practice:** Work as though success depended entirely upon your efforts – pray as though success depended upon God alone.

಄಑ఞ❀ಚಾಜ

### 320 ~ Thursday

**"And which of you by taking thought can add to his stature one cubit?"**
**~ St. Matthew (6:27)**

**Thought:** What is here said of the body is true also of the soul. Unless God aids me in my endeavours, I can increase neither in wisdom nor in virtue. All that is positive, real, true, and good within me comes from God. I can co-operate with the Divine action. I may even resist it; but without God I can do nothing.

**Prayer:** Jesus, I delight in acknowledging that without Thee I am utterly powerless. To whom can I better confide my interests either for time or eternity, for body or soul, than to Thee, O Lord?

**Practice:** Faithfulness to grace.

಄಑ఞ❀ಚಾಜ

## 321 ~Friday

**"For your Father knoweth that you have need of all these things." ~ St. Matthew (6:32)**

**Thought:** He knows this and He is desirous of procuring them for you; but He wishes to be asked for them, He expects homage and acknowledgement of your dependence. When you have prayed and worked, or rather during your prayer and work, abandon yourself to His wisdom, bounty, and power. Await His time with confidence and patience.

**Prayer:** Jesus, Thou knowest my needs. Thou knowest my desires. Thou wilt forget neither the one nor the other.

**Practice:** Confidence in God in spite of everything.

৩৩৩৩❈৩৩৩৩

## 322 ~Saturday

**"Seek ye therefore first the kingdom of God and His justice, and all these things shall be added unto you." ~ St. Matthew (6:33)**

**Thought:** The Church is the kingdom of God here on earth. Let us work and combat, live and die for the Church; forgetting self and all things else, thinking only of God and His interests: then God will not forget us and our interests.

**Prayer:** Jesus, be Thou the only object of my care. Thy reign once secure, my destiny will also be secure.

**Practice:** Cause Jesus to reign firstly over yourself, and afterwards over all those who are under your influence.

ಜಜ⊕ಚಚಜಜ⊕ಚಚಜಜ⊕ಚಚ

## 323 ~ Fifteenth Sunday After Pentecost

**"Jesus went into a city that is called Naim; and there went with Him His disciples and a great multitude." ~ St. Luke (7:11)**

**Thought:** A great multitude follows Jesus, though He Himself never seeks popularity. For thirty years He has lived unknown. Whenever He is able, He retires into solitude. Let us fly the crowd, let us not seek popularity. Let us speak and do well; the people will listen to us when God wills it.

**Prayer:** Jesus, forgetful of Thy own glory, Thou seekest only the glory of The Father, yet is glory rendered to Thee. I would forget myself for Thee, I desire no glory save Thine.

**Practice**: Fly from the crowd.

ಜಜ⊕ಚಚ

**"A dead man was carried out, the only son of his mother, and she was a widow."**
**~ St. Luke (7:12)**

**Thought:** The Church is a mother, and like to a widow by the absence of her heavenly Spouse. The sinner is her son. Although he is not an only son, she mourns over him as such. And whilst the Church weeps over the sinner, he is buried in those passions which drag him towards base material things.

**Prayer:** Jesus, do not permit me to be carried away by sensible and sensual things.

**Practice:** Call upon Jesus when you feel yourself overcome by passion.

ಉಞ❀ಚಚ

## 325 ~ Tuesday

**"Whom when the Lord had seen, being moved with mercy towards her, He said to her; Weep not." ~ St. Luke (7:13)**

**Thought:** Jesus has compassion, even on our temporal sorrows. When He allows us to suffer, it is for our good. But we may without offending Him, have recourse to His goodness in worldly trials as well as in spiritual affliction.  We shall be heard and rewarded according as it may be most advantageous to us.

**Prayer:** Jesus, why do I so often forget Thy goodness to think only of Thy justice?

**Practice:** Confidence in the goodness of the Heart of Jesus.

ಖಣ⊛ಣಞ

## 326 ~ Wednesday

### "And He came and touched the bier."
### ~ St. Luke (7:14)

**Thought:** God draws near unto the dead man, for the dead cannot approach Him.  Thus when a soul is dead to God by sin, it will never be able to approach God, unless He draws near by His grace.  God is Mercy itself; He draws near and touches the bier.  He stops the bearers, i.e., the passions which were dragging the soul down to its infernal sepulchre.

**Prayer:** Jesus, do Thou but touch this garb of death which surrounds me.  Inaction paralyses my mind, coldness freezes my heart.  Touch my mind by Thy Word, and my heart by Thy grace, and I shall regain the activity and ardour of supernatural life.

**Practice:** Respond to the first advances of grace.

ಖಣ⊛ಣಞ

## 327 ~ Thursday

### "Young man I say to thee, Arise."
### ~ St. Luke (7:14)

**Thought:** One word of Jesus sufficed to give life to the dead. One word sufficed Him to draw from nothingness worlds of matter and mind. One word also suffices Him to give back to the soul the life of grace; but the soul on her part must act according to the words of her Master – *surge*, arise – as if He had said – I give thee back the power to rise, but thou must use that power. I give thee the power of detesting sin and correcting thyself of it, but thou must avail thyself of this power. God created us without ourselves, but He will not save us without our co-operation. - (St. Augustine.)

**Prayer:** Jesus, say unto me one of those words which transforms, elevates, and restores life.

**Practice:** Faithfulness to grace.

ಐಐ✿ಲಚ

## 328 ~ Friday

### "And he that was dead sat up and began to speak." ~ St. Luke (7:15)

**Thought:** Do at least what lies in your power. If it seems impossible for you to stand upright, at least make the effort. You cannot, you say, give up this or that sinful practice. You can at least pray, and you can speak to God, the Blessed Virgin, and the saints – *et coepit loqui.* God by His grace will do the rest.

**Prayer:** Jesus, I will make an effort when Thou callest, with the certainty that my effort will be seconded by new graces, more efficacious than former graces.

**Practice:** Pray as soon as you are able, i.e., always.

ೞಚಾ✿ಚಾಚ

## 329 ~ Saturday

**"A great prophet is risen up among us."**
**~ St. Luke (7:16)**

**Thought:** Man is known by his works better even than by his words. He who works supernaturally must speak in words not less supernatural. Jesus performs a miracle, and the people conclude that He is a prophet. They are only mistaken in not fully realising it. The Christian lives supernaturally, especially by Holy Communion. Are you known as a Christian by your conduct and your speech?

**Prayer:** Jesus, grant that united to Thee by Baptism and Communion, I may honour Thee and show myself Thy disciple by the dignity of my conversation.

**Practice:** Show yourself worthy of Jesus.

289

ಐ೫⊛ಐ೮೫ಐ೫⊛ಐ೮೫ಐ೫⊛ಐ೮

## 330 ~ Sixteenth Sunday After Pentecost

**"Jesus went into the house of one of the chief of the Pharisees on the Sabbath day to eat bread, and they watched Him."**
**~ St. Luke (14:1)**

**Thought:** Jesus can do nothing without being criticised; yet you hope to escape censure? If everybody thinks well of you, you are not the disciple of Jesus. Universal favour is only obtained by universal flattery. If you please everybody, how many passions and prejudices do you not satisfy? And this, being the case, you could not satisfy honest, sensible persons; therefore it is impossible to please everybody.

**Prayer:** Jesus, teach me to despise censure as Thou didst despise it.

**Practice:** Be above censure.

ಐ೫⊛ಐ೮

## 331 ~Monday

**"And behold there was a certain man before Him that had the dropsy."**
**~ St. Luke (14:2)**

**Thought:** This swelling is symbolical of pride, and also of science (knowledge) which when not moderated by humility, swells the mind and the heart. This man with the dropsy is a living type of those Pharisees who watched Jesus that they might find Him in fault and thus console the pride of their false science and virtue, so often confounded by the wisdom of the Saviour.

**Prayer:** Jesus, I stand before Thee with my vanity and my swellings; Thou alone canst cure me.

**Practice:** Esteem not yourself above your worth.

ಜಙ✿ಐದ

## 332 ~ Tuesday

### "Is it lawful to heal on the Sabbath day?"<br>~ St. Luke (14:3)

**Thought:** Jesus needs neither the answer of the doctors to know what is lawful, nor the permission of the Pharisees to heal the infirm. The question, then, is ironical. He who by one word can cure the sick surely knows the law as well as the doctors. The law forbids servile works. Miracles are Divine works. But Jesus mocks the Pharisees and their overweening pride.

**Prayer:** Jesus, teach me to despise false knowledge and the bad intentions of my enemies.

**Practice:** Confound the enemies of Jesus Christ by word and action.

ಜಙ✿ಐದ

## 333 ~ Wednesday

### "But they held their peace." ~ St. Luke (14:4)

**Thought:** Rather than recognise and declare the truth, the false doctors are silent. It is the rule with sophists as well as with politicians to abstain from giving a solution, that they may reserve to themselves a pretext wherewith to surprise and condemn their adversary.

**Prayer:** Jesus, at every moment of my life, I meet with bad faith and intrigue which oppose me in my good designs. Thou, O Lord, hast met with the same difficulties, but Thou didst never waver in pursuit of Thy object.

**Practice:** Despise equally the silence and the converse of enemies to good, and continue your work.

ಜ಼ಌ❀ಌಚ

## 334 ~ Thursday

### "But Jesus, taking him, healed him and sent him away." ~ St. Luke (14:4)

**Thought:** Do good in spite of everything. If you are forbidden by man to speak, or do anything for the glory of God or the salvation of souls (though Christ Himself has charged you with this mission through His Church), persevere, and take upon yourselves that liberty which is refused you; it is your right.

**Prayer:** Jesus, after silencing Thy enemies by a simple question, Thou didst bring confusion upon them by the greatness of Thy action; teach us to imitate Thee and confound the world by words of faith and works of charity.

**Practice:** Put a stop to ungodliness by the practice of charity.

ಜ಼ಜ಼ ✦ ಜ಼ಜ಼

### 335 ~ Friday

**"And they could not answer Him to these things."** ~ St. Luke (14:3)

**Thought:** What could they answer? If Jesus speaks He outdoes in wisdom these cunning and clever men by one simple question. His actions show Him to be a prophet, a messenger from God – God Himself. Bow down, oh ye proud spirits, and acknowledge your Master. This is the answer which you could and ought to make, but pride refuses to submit.

**Prayer:** Jesus, I rejoice that Thou dost triumph over Thy enemies. Grant that I may assist as much as I am able in they combats and victories.

**Practice:** Combat the enemies of Jesus by works as well as by words.

ಜ಼ಜ಼ ✦ ಜ಼ಜ಼

## 336 ~ Saturday

**"Every one that exalteth himself shall be humbled, and he that humbleth himself shall be exalted."** ~ St. Luke (14:11)

**Thought:** Even humanly speaking, humility is the surest means of arriving at glory; for even in this world, pride ends only in confusion. Besides, why care about the esteem or contempt of men who are so blind, so unjust in their judgement? They are annoyed at the sight of true merit, and they only grant honour to those on whose servility they can depend. *In fine*, the world esteems those whom it appears to contemn, and despises those whom it seems to honour.

**Prayer:** Jesus, teach me sincerely to despise the world and public opinion; I shall only be truly happy when I feel desirous to be forgotten altogether by the world.

**Practice:** Seek obscurity, solitude, and the lowest place.

කුණු ✤ ලැවූ කුණු ✤ ලැවූ කුණු ✤ ලැවූ

## 337 ~ Seventeenth Sunday After Pentecost

**"But the Pharisees, hearing He had silenced the Sadducees, came together."**
~ St. Matthew (22:34)

**Thought:** They do not unite in search of truth,

but to destroy Jesus, who is Truth itself.  Thus are united the enemies of the Church, not through love of truth, but through hatred of the incorruptible, infallible guardian of truth.

**Prayer:** Jesus, grant that as the wicked are assembled against Thee, so the good may unite around Thee.

**Practice:** Let us be united with the Pope who is Vicar of Christ by docility of faith, and we shall be united both to Jesus Christ and to one another in truth of which the Pope is the infallible teacher.

ಬಙ❀ಞ೮ಚ

### 338 ~ Monday

**"Master, which is the great commandment of the law?"** ~ St. Matthew (22:36)

**Thought:**  There is a snare in the simple manner of the question.  But the snare is broken by the simplicity of the answer.  Let us distrust the apparent candour of the enemies of faith, especially when they feign ignorance or when they address us with pompous titles.  Let us destroy their malice by the firmness and straightforwardness of our answer.

**Prayer:** Jesus, Thou art truly Master, and Thy answer goes to prove it.  Be Thou my light and my strength.

**Practice:** Uprightness and simplicity of word and action.

෨෫෨෯ඓ

### 339 ~ Tuesday

**"Thou shalt love the Lord thy God with thy whole heart, and with thy whole soul, and with thy whole mind." ~ St. Matthew (22:37)**

**Thought:** *Diliges*—Thou shalt love – love of preference, deliberate love directed by the mind, not passionate or instinctive love. God is my Master, to Him I owe everything. *Dominum* – Lord, this Master is my God and the supreme Good. *Deum* – God. He deserves all my love.

**Prayer:** Jesus, teach me to love Thee with my whole heart. Once enlightened by faith and understanding, my heart will place at Thy feet my soul and all its powers, my mind and all its intentions.

**Practice:** Hold nothing in your heart that tends not to God.

෨෫෨෯ඓ

### 340 ~ Wednesday

**"This is the greatest and first commandment."
~ St. Matthew (22:38)**

**Thought:** This is the first commandment,

because it is the principle whence springs all the other commandments; the *greatest* commandment, because in it all others are contained. He that loves God desires all that God desires. He that loves God with all his heart prefers God to every other good.

**Prayer:** Jesus, instead of making numberless intentions, I will think, wish for, and love only one thing, the glory of Thy heavenly Father and the means of serving Him.

**Practice:** Have God always in sight.

ജ∞❀ଔ੪

## 341 ~ Thursday

**"And the second is like to this, thou shalt love thy neighbour as thyself."**
**~ St. Matthew (22:39)**

**Thought:** If I love God I shall love my neighbour, because like myself he is the work of God, the image of God, and the child of God. If I love myself I shall love my brother, he is like to me. This second commandment is like to the first, just as our neighbour is like to God.

**Prayer:** Jesus, Thy love for man was such that Thou didst make him like to Thee, and Thou lovest him as much as, and in one sense, more than Thyself; for Thou didst sacrifice Thyself for him. Teach me Thy lesson and example.

**Practice:** Brotherly charity.

ಜು<svm>ಖ೧✿ಛಲಚ

### 342 ~ Friday

**"In these two commandments depend the whole law and the prophets."**
**~ St. Matthew (22:40)**

**Thought:** The law informs us what ought to be done, but prophets tell us what will be done. To love God and our neighbour is what we should so, and this will be done, for the prophets have announced Jesus Christ. Thus to speak of Jesus is to tell of love for God and neighbour, of love, even unto death upon the Cross, for God and souls.

**Prayer:** Jesus, fill me with that double love which causes Thy Heart to beat, and which gives Thee to us as our Saviour and our King.

**Practice:** Love of God whom you see not, by the love of your neighbour whom you see.

ಜುಖ೧✿ಛಲಚ

### 343 ~ Saturday

**"And no man was able to answer Him a word."**
**~ St. Matthew (22:46)**

**Thought:** Jesus silences His enemies thereby giving an example to His Church and His ministers,

298

who live only in order to obtain for truth and justice the victory over falsehood and iniquity. But we must be patient, humble, and charitable. Patience consists in suffering death rather than betray the cause of truth and justice; humility consists in submitting to truth by faith, to the commandments by obedience in repelling all liberty which is based upon falsehood or injustice; charity bids us enlighten those who teach falsehood and are ignorant of what is right.

**Prayer:** Jesus, give me a little of that eloquence and wisdom with which Thou didst confound falsehood and unmask ignorance.

**Practice:** Study your religion that you may be in a position to defend it.

## 344 ~ Eighteenth Sunday After Pentecost

**"And entering into a boat He passed over the water and came into His own city."**
**~ St. Matthew (9:1)**

**Thought:** Jesus comes into His own city. We are then permitted to remember our relations but it must be as Jesus remembered them, that we may enlighten them by our discourse and bring them to God, by our works and by our example.

**Prayer:** Jesus, transform the natural feelings of my heart, even those most legitimate, into supernatural sentiments. Grant that I may love my neighbour for Thy sake alone.

**Practice:** Above and before all, seek the glory of God.

ಬಙ❀ಞಬ

### 345 ~ Monday

**"And behold they brought to Him one sick of the palsy, lying in a bed." ~ St. Matthew (9:2)**

**Thought:** If I am deprived of strength and energy, what can I do for God and my neighbour? And I am discouraged by the impotence of my efforts, by uselessness of my works, I am sick and prostrate. Jesus is the giver of all strength, why, then, do I not present myself to Him?

**Prayer:** Jesus, behold me stretched motionless at Thy feet; Thou canst give me that supernatural life and strength which fail me now.

**Practice:** Expect help from Jesus only.

ಬಙ❀ಞಬ

"And Jesus, seeing their faith, said to the man sick of the palsy, Be of good heart, son, they sins are forgiven thee."
~ St. Matthew (9:3)

**Thought:** Faith does not go unrewarded. It obtains all things, more even than it asks for, and obtains even when apparently it asks for nothing. What did they who brought the man sick of the palsy? They laid him at the feet of Jesus without saying a word. Jesus understood them. They expected the cure of this sick man; they will obtain it and more, even. Jesus goes back to the primary cause of all infirmities – *Sin.* He begins by forgiving the sick man his sins. Spiritual cure before bodily cure; but the body does not lose by it.

**Prayer:** Jesus, take pity on my spiritual misery, which is generally the cause of my temporal misery, and of the impotence of my words and actions.

**Practice:** Begin by purifying your conscience.

ಜುಜ಼ು ✸ ಞಜಚ಼

### 347 ~ Wednesday

"And behold some of the Scribes said within themselves, He blasphemeth."
~ St. Matthew (9:3)

**Thought:** The enemy is always on the watch ready to criticism and condemn all that Jesus may do and say. This disciple is not greater than the Master. Let us then be resigned and bear censure, blame, and condemnation; but whatever may happen, whatever may be said, we should never tire of speaking truth and doing good.

**Prayer:** Jesus, teach me to take no heed of those discontented jealous minds whose only happiness is to censure.

**Practice:** Let us lift ourselves above the annoyances stirred up by pride and envy.

ॐ⊕ॐ

## 348 ~ Thursday

**"And Jesus seeing their thoughts said, Why do you think evil in your hearts."**
**~ St. Matthew (9:1)**

**Thought:** Let us follow the example of Jesus, and allow no attack from the enemy to pass unanswered. It is both just and charitable of us to do so – just towards the aggressor, for our silence would but confirm his prejudice; just to those who have read or heard of the lies of the impious, otherwise our silence would be taken as an avowal and calumny would pass as truth; charitable towards the enemies of truth in taking trouble to enlighten them; charitable towards those who would be dupes to untruth and sophism if we did not confound the liar and the sophist. But we must persevere to the end. We must penetrate to the thoughts of the enemy, and even unmask the motive – *Ut quid cogitatis mala in cardibus vestris.* Let us remember, however, that there may be cases in which silence is more eloquent and more startling than speech.

**Prayer:** Jesus, give me one virtue more heroic even than patience which submits to everything; grant me sufficient courage to attack error and vice; give me strength to combat what is false and evil.

**Practice:** Defend Jesus when He is attacked in the person of His Church and ministers.

಼ಜ಼✠ಣಜ

## 349 ~ Friday

**"Rise, take up thy bed and go into thy house."**
**~ St. Matthew (9:6)**

**Thought:** Jesus adds action to the word, and thus confounds the malice of His enemies. We must not leave any attack against religion unanswered, but our actions must be in accordance with our words. The enemy of God particularly wishes to prevent our acting. Let us then *speak* well and boldly, but especially let us *do* well in spite of everything.

**Prayer:** Jesus, grant me courage both in words and actions. Command. There is strength in Thy command, and it is communicated to him who, in obedience, tries to rise and walk.

**Practice:** Do your best – God will do the rest.

໖໐໖❀໖໐໖

### 350 ~ Saturday

**"And the multitude seeing it, feared and glorified God."** ~ St. Matthew (9:8)

**Thought:** It purports nothing, men will say, to combat and confound the enemies of the Church if you do not convert them. To which I reply, were you to convert but one soul all your trouble would be sufficiently repaid. But we have not only to convert the enemy, but also to preserve and strengthen those whom the enemy will deceive, unless his teaching be unmasked and he himself be reduced to silence. Jesus did not convert the Scribes whom He confounded, but He enlightened the people upon the dangers of their doctrines.

**Prayer:** Jesus, give to my words and actions strength to confound the wicked, and to help simple and upright souls.

**Practice:** Never cease to combat.

໖໐໖❀໖໐໖

ಙಞ✲ಚಿ೦ಶಙಞ✲ಚಿ೦ಶಙಞ✲ಚಿ೦ಶ

## 351 ~Nineteenth Sunday After Pentecost

**"The kingdom of heaven is likened to a king who made a marriage for his son."**
**~ St. Matthew (22:1)**

**Thought:** God the Father celebrates the alliance of His Son with humanity. We are invited to partake of this alliance by Holy Communion. This union constitutes the reign of God over souls, and this reign offers us the certainty of happiness and eternal life.

**Prayer:** Jesus, grant that I may understand and participate in the dignity and blessedness to which I am so touchingly invited by Thy heavenly Father.

**Practice:** Thank God incessantly because He has deigned to come down to us, that He might raise us up to Him.

ಙಞ✲ಚಿ೦ಶ

## 352 ~ Monday

**"And he sent his servants to call them that were invited to the marriage, and they would not come."** ~ St. Matthew (22:2)

**Thought:** God sent His prophets to call the Jews to the marriage feast. Jesus Himself sent the apostles to draw thither the Gentiles, but a small number only answered this glorious invitation. Each day am I invited by the secret inspiration of grace, and I am generally deaf to the invitation, or I openly resist it.

**Prayer:** Jesus, when shall I promptly, entirely, and with constancy reply to Thy call?

**Practice:** Be faithful to all the inspirations of grace.

ಙಞ❀ಞಙ

### 353 ~ Tuesday

**"They went their ways, one to his farm, and another to his merchandise."**
**~ St. Matthew (22:5)**

**Thought:** Men of the world neglect God, some for pleasure, others for the sake of business. And I, where do I find my pleasure? Is it in union with God through prayer and Communion? What is my most important business? Is it the glory of God, the salvation of my soul, and that of my neighbours?

**Prayer:** Jesus, at Thy call, I abandon everything. What pleasure can be greater than to be united to Thee? What business, what interest, is worth one single Communion?

**Practice:** Renounce everything and follow Jesus.

ಜಜಾ❀ಡಿಡಿ

## 354 ~ Wednesday

**"But when the king heard of it, he was angry, and sending his armies, he destroyed those murderers, and burned their city."**
**~ St. Matthew (22:7)**

**Thought:** Not content with refusing his invitation, they murdered the king's servants. These sinners who, not satisfied with refusing grace, hunt out and kill the servants of God when they can do so. But woe to them, they will lose the grace that they refuse as well as those false advantages which they prefer to grace.

**Prayer:** Jesus, in spite of all opposition, Thou wilt reign in this life and in the next. Commence at once Thy reign over my heart.

**Practice:** Voluntary submission to the good pleasure of God.

ಜಜಾ❀ಡಿಡಿ

## 355 ~ Thursday

**"Go ye therefore into the highways, and as many as you shall find, call to the marriage."** ~ **St. Matthew (22:9)**

**Thought:** Jesus will call a certain number of elect, whom in His eternal decrees He has determined upon. If you refuse the honour done to you in being invited to the Divine banquet, God will do without you, your place will easily be filled. If stones only could be found He is able to change them into the children of Abraham. Then, will narrow-minded, hard-hearted, vulgar minds become suddenly changed, and they will take the place of those chosen, noble-minded, high-souled Christians who have refused the Divine invitation.

**Prayer:** Jesus, Thou didst meet me on the roadside when I was hastening to perdition. Thou hast called me to replace some great being who has disdained Thy advances. Grant that I may not become unworthy of Thy favours.

**Practice:** Have a childlike fear of losing grace.

ಜಲ⊛ಲ⊛

### 356 ~ Friday

**"Friend, how camest thou in thither, not having on a wedding garment."**
**~ St. Matthew (22:12)**

**Thought:** One must be worthy to assist at this royal banquet. Sinner! The angels and ministers of God have met thee on the road to death and perdition. Come with full detestation of sin. Thou hast indeed lost the white robe of baptism, but clothe thyself now in the garb of penance.

**Prayer:** Jesus, I pray Thee, not only call me to Thee, but purify me in Thy Blood, render me worthy to receive Thee in Communion.

**Practice:** Retain the grace of purity by frequent examinations of conscience.

ꕤ

## 357 ~ Saturday

**"For many are called, but few are chosen." ~ St. Matthew (22:14)**

**Thought:** Many are invited, but few reply to the call. Pleasures and earthly interests engage us more than that joy and glory which will be eternal, which is to come. Worldly festivals and worldly interests are preferred before God. Thus do we lose both our soul and God.

**Prayer:** Jesus, call me, draw me towards Thee. If I resist, use gentle violence to save me in spite of myself.

**Practice:** Be with the small number – the multitude will be lost.

ꕤ

## 358 ~ Twentieth Sunday After Pentecost

**"He came again into Cana of Galilee where He had made the water wine."**
**~ St. John (4:46)**

**Thought:** One is pleased to return to a place where one has done good, but when we return we must, like Jesus, intend to do a greater good.

**Prayer:** Jesus, Thou didst change the water into wine, change Thou my weakness into strength, work this miracle in my soul, O Lord.

**Practice:** If you are unable to do all that you wish, do at least all you can. Offer water if you have nothing better, leaving it to Jesus to change the water into wine.

## 359 ~ Monday

**"And a certain ruler went to Him and prayed Him to come down and heal his son."**
**~ St. John (4:46-47)**

**Thought:** This young man was at death's door. In dire extremity have recourse to Jesus and you shall live. If everything seems lost, Jesus by one word can repair it all. Speak but one word, and Jesus will show Himself to you.

**Prayer:** Jesus, I know that I am powerless; for the future I will have recourse to Thee in all my troubles.

**Practice:** Invoke Jesus in time of temptation and affliction.

ॐ❀ॐ

## 360 ~ Tuesday

**"Unless you see signs and wonders you believe not." ~ St. John (4:48)**

**Thought:** Why seek for wonders? Follow in the common path, look at Jesus. He is not less admirable nor is His Divinity shown less brilliantly in His ordinary life than in the miracles He performs. Be dignified and simple in all your actions, then whatever you do, you will be like Jesus, *great*.

**Prayer:** Jesus, teach me that true greatness does not consist in doing much, but in doing well.

**Practice:** Follow the example shown you by Jesus, perform all your actions well.

ॐ❀ॐ

## 361 ~ Wednesday

**"Lord, come down before that my son die."**
**~ St. John (4:49)**

**Thought:** In spite of this, the father repeats his prayer. He wishes to save his son. No real or apparent obstacles can disconcert him. When God seems obstinate in His refusal, persist in your demand – prayer overcomes all things.

**Prayer:** Jesus, I will not cease praying to Thee until I have completely realised those designs which I have conceived for Thy glory.

**Practice:** Constancy and confidence in prayer. Persevere until you have triumphed.

ಜಿ೫ಿ❀ఇ౪

## 362 ~ Thursday

**"Go thy way, thy son liveth." ~ St. John (4:50)**

**Thought:** Through faith we obtain all things. It may happen that you receive no temporal blessings, but in their stead grace far superior will be granted you. Ask especially that your soul may live, and your prayers will be heard.

**Prayer:** Jesus, when wilt Thou say to me – Go, have no further care, thy soul liveth and is cured of such a vice, of such a fault? When I have united prayer to earnest endeavour.

**Practice:** Work and pray, pray and work – this is the secret of life.

ಞಞ✹ಞಞ

## 363 ~ Friday

**"The man believed the word which Jesus said to him, and went his way."**
**~ St. John (4:50)**

**Thought:** When Jesus speaks to you, either by a direct command from your superiors or by inspirations of grace, do not hesitate – believe and go. But it is incredible, impossible! Go. What seems impossible will become a reality, what appears incredible will become an established fact when Jesus shall have spoken. This man had not reached his home before the servants met him with the news that his son was restored to health.

**Prayer:** Jesus, inspire me with prompt and lively faith, so that I may receive Thy orders and inspirations without hesitation.

**Practice:** Prompt and simple obedience to the will of God whenever it is manifested to you.

ಞಞ✹ಞಞ

## 364 ~ Saturday

### "And himself believed and his whole house."
### ~ St. John (4:53)

**Thought:**  There are several degrees of faith. Just now, this prince simply believed in the word of the Saviour telling him of the cure of his son. Now that with his own eyes he has witnessed the truth in which he had believed, before his faith becomes greater and more widely spread – greater, for he now believes in the Almighty power and the Divinity of Jesus, more widely-spread inasmuch as it is communicated by him to all his household.

**Prayer:** Jesus, I believe, but increase my faith, grant that by my fidelity to the first glimpses of faith, I may deserve complete enlightenment.

**Practice:** Docility to the impulse of grace.

ಜಞ ✤ ಲ೮ಜಞ ✤ ಲ೮ಜಞ ✤ ಲ೮

## 365 ~ Twenty-First Sunday After Pentecost

### "Therefore is the kingdom of heaven likened to a king who would take an account of his servants." ~ St. Matthew (18:2)

**Thought:** God will demand of me an account of how I have used all that He confided to me, body, soul, intelligence, will, senses, health, strength, worldly goods, natural and supernatural gifts. Every thought, every desire, every word will be examined and judged. Recompense or punishment will be awarded. I must render an account of every useless word that I have spoken.

**Prayer:** Jesus, Thou who wilt be my Judge, grant me grace to forestall Thy judgements by daily examination of conscience made in Thy presence as though Thou wert already judging me.

**Practice:** Examine your conscience every evening.

ಜಜ⊛ಞಟ

## 366 ~ Monday

**"Have patience with me, and I will pay thee all." ~ St. Matthew (18:26)**

**Thought:** Alas! For how many years has not Jesus borne with me! Year after year, I rob Him of His due. All my thoughts, desires, words, and actions should tend towards His greater glory, and I use all these for my own profit, or rather for my own loss. I think only of myself, I love only myself, and my conversation always tends to my own personal advantage; I work only for my own interest. And God has not yet taken from me the use of my senses and my faculties. He snatches me not from the life which I abuse. How great is His patience!

**Prayer:** Jesus, be patient a little longer; for the future I will do all for the glory of Thee.

**Practice:** Often offer yourself up to God.

ಖಜಾ❀ಠಜಿಡ

### 367 ~ Tuesday

**"And the lord of that servant, being moved with pity, let him go, and forgave him the debt."** ~ **St. Matthew (18:27)**

**Thought:** God not only bears with me and continues His favour toward me, but also keeps me in His service in spite of my oft-renewed wanderings from Him; and if I only acknowledge my infidelity and my ingratitude, He forgets the past and confers upon me new graces for the future.

**Prayer:** Jesus, if the Heavenly Father forgives me my debt thus easily, it is because Thou hast paid my debt with Thy own Blood. To Thee, then, am I indebted! May I never forget that I am Thy debtor now and for all eternity.

**Practice:** Make up for lost time, and do everything for the service of God.

ಖಜಾ❀ಠಜಿಡ

## 368 ~ Wednesday

**"And laying hold of him he throttled him, saying, Pay what thou owest."**
**~ St. Matthew (18:28)**

**Thought:** We always find a thousand excellent excuses for our gravest faults, but if any one wrong us in the least, the offence at once becomes unpardonable. We have a thousand reasons wherewith to condemn our neighbour, but not one wherewith to excuse him.

**Prayer:** Jesus, Thou who didst find excuses for those who nailed Thee to the Cross, teach me to understand that true superiority and real greatness of soul consists in forgetting injury, and in being above insult.

**Practice:** Pardon and forget injuries.

ಜುಜು❀ಞಞ

## 369 ~ Thursday

**"Now his fellow-servants, seeing what was done, were very much grieved."**
**~ St. Matthew (18:31)**

**Thought:** Nothing inures us so much in the eyes of our neighbours as that pitiless severity which renders us exacting, difficult to please and implacable. He who can bear nothing is himself unbearable. We do not forgive that man who forgives nobody.

**Prayer:** Jesus, grant that I may not sadden my brethren by my intolerance towards those who offend me: may I remember that I have defects for which I claim indulgence.

**Practice:** Close the eye to the defects of others, and open it to your own.

ಬಾ🕸ೞಯ

### 370 ~ Friday

**"And his lord being angry, delivered him to the torturers until he paid all the debt."**
**~ St. Matthew (18:34)**

**Thought:** How can you deserve pity if you show none to your neighbour? Be not too exacting if you are desirous that God should not be so to you. The thought of purgatory frightens you, and not without reason. There you will have to expiate everything, even the idly spoken word. Forgive then, and remit what is owing to you, that God may forgive you your debt. The great secret of escape from the flames of purgatory is the forgiveness of injuries.

**Prayer:** Jesus, soften my heart by the sight of Thy Heart; teach me to forget and pardon all the injuries I have ever received.

**Practice:** Think of the severity of Divine Judgement, and you will be less severe in your judgement of others.

ಬಾ🕸ೞಯ

## 371 ~ Saturday

**"So also shall my Heavenly Father do to you, if you forgive not every one his brother from your hearts."** ~ St. Matthew (18:35)

**Thought:** After all, what are the offences committed against us in comparison with those we are guilty of towards God? Generally the injury is only imaginary. The offender had not even the intention of hurting us. Often, too, we take as an injury truth which is spoken of us, an act of justice which is rendered to us. *In fine*, it rarely happens that the offence causes us a real loss, one affecting the soul, or compromising our eternal interests.

**Prayer**: Jesus, teach me how wrong it is of me, after offending Goodness Itself, to be so sensible of an offence which really benefits more than it injures.

**Practice:** Look upon offences as a means of expiation and reparation for your own faults.

ಜ಼ಾ ✤ ಲ಼ಚ

## 372 ~ Twenty-Second Sunday
## After Pentecost

"Then the Pharisees, going consulted among themselves how to ensnare Him in His speech." ~ St. Matthew (22:15)

**Thought:** If you proclaim the truth and do good actions you offend the wicked, and never afterwards will you be able to take a step or say a word without being watched, commented upon, wrongly interpreted, and denounced before those who have power to silence you. Be careful, then, in your speech, and keep watch upon your actions; be irreproachable.

**Prayer:** Jesus, why should I wonder or be vexed that I am a butt for criticism, when Thou couldst not go unscathed?

**Practice:** Be careful in speech and action, that you may not be entrapped by malice.

ಬುಕಾ ✹ ಲ೨ಲಙ

## 373 ~ Monday

"And they sent to Him their disciples with the Herodians." ~ St. Matthew (22:16)

**Thought:** Those Pharisees who were so proud,

so imbued with a sense of their authority, must have hated the partisans of Herod. The sceptre of this king and stranger to their nation must have weighed as heavily upon them as the Roman yoke. Yet they join with the enemies of their country and their religion, with those who are hostile to their power; they unite with them and plot the perdition of Him Who alone can and would save and enfranchise Israel, Who alone can and will give to her people and her chiefs power stronger far than that worldly and political power of the Herods and the Caesars.

**Prayer:** Jesus, Thou alone by Thy Church grantest true liberty to nations; thou givest to rulers a sway mild and strong. In spite of this, nations and rulers stand in league against Thee and Thy Church. Jealousy is so blind!

**Practice:** For the sake of Jesus and His Church, cross swords with sophists and politicians.

๛๛✺ඏൠ

### 374 ~ Tuesday

**"Master, we know that Thou art a true speaker, and teachest the way of God in truth, neither carest Thou for any man."**
**~ St. Matthew (22:16)**

**Thought:** Mistrust those who praise you much, even though the praises be your due. It is a snare which through your simplicity is laid to entrap you. They may exalt your truthfulness, your impartiality,

321

but only that they may obtain from you a word against authority, a word contrary to charity, a word that may compromise and ensure your fall.

**Prayer:**  Jesus, teach me to be indifferent to praise, grant that I may never be dazzled by it.

**Practice:** Mistrust flattery.


ಜಞ೫ೞಚ


## 375 ~ Wednesday

**"Tell us therefore what Thou dost think, is it lawful to give tribute to Caesar or not?"**
**~ St. Matthew (22:17)**


**Thought:** The snare is laid with admirable precision.  If Jesus answers, "It is permitted to give tribute to Caesar," they will denounce Him as having recognised the rule of Rome over Judea, and therefore as an enemy to His country.  If He says – It is not permitted to give tribute, they will denounce Him to the lieutenant of Caesar.  The Herodians are there, ready to hand Him over to the power which supports their king.  This will often be the position of the Church in the world.

**Prayer:** Jesus, grant me prudence in dealing with those who only seek to compromise the preachers of the Gospel and the defenders of the Church.

**Practice:** Be circumspect in your relations with worldly men.

৪০৪০ ✿ ০৪০৪

### 376 ~ Thursday

**"But Jesus, knowing their wickedness, said, Why do you tempt Me, ye hypocrites?"**
**~ St. Matthew (22:81)**

**Thought:** Unmask the hypocrite, let him know that he is found out. The simplicity of the dove is useless without the prudence of the serpent. Humility, mildness and charity should not prevent us from calling things and persons by their rights names. Love one another, but detest the hypocrite. Learn of Jesus. He is meek and humble of heart, but He does not hesitate to unmask the hypocrite.

**Prayer:** Jesus, teach me to be simple but prudent; mild, but bold; humble but free like Thee.

**Practice:** Uphold truth and right, fear not to wound the politician who seeks to suppress the one and the other.

৪০৪০ ✿ ০৪০৪

## 377 ~ Friday

## "Whose image and inscription is this?"
## ~ St. Matthew (22:20)

**Thought:**  Whose image and inscription are those engraved upon your heart?  Are they the image and inscription of Caesar, the prince of this world?  Yes, if your thoughts and aspirations tend only towards the worldly goods and pleasures and honours which belong to Caesar and are granted by him.  Then you are a slave and tributary to Caesar, i.e., to whoever is powerful in this world.  Yet in spite of all that you can do, you will never efface the marks of the image of God in you; you will never be able to forget His Name, or that law which He has engraved in the bottom of your soul to enlighten and guide you, and by which you will be judged and condemned.

**Prayer:** Jesus, reinstate the Divine likeness in my soul, engrave upon it Thy Name and the Name of Thy Father.

**Practice:**  Keep always within your mind the image and Name of God by imitating His Divine perfection and by repeating the Divine Name.

ಬಾಣ ✵ ೞಉ

## 378 ~ Saturday

"Render therefore to Caesar the things that are Caesar's, and to God the things that are God's." ~ St. Matthew (22:21)

**Thought:** Give every one his due. Give to Caesar tribute and temporal and worldly homage; to God the homage of ourselves, all that we are, all that we have, all that we are able to do. Give only temporal homage to Caesar, but to God give temporal as well as spiritual homage, body as well as soul, exterior as well as interior tribute. God has absolute and entire right to everything in us and around us.

**Prayer:** Jesus, Thou art almighty upon earth, as in heaven, may Thy kingdom come, Thy will be done upon earth as it is in heaven.

**Practice:** Acknowledge God as the source of everything.

ಋಕ﹡ಡಉಋಕ﹡ಡಉಋಕ﹡ಡಉ

## 379 ~ Twenty-Third Sunday After Pentecost

"Behold a certain ruler came up and adored Him." ~ St. Matthew (9:18)

**Thought:** Are you in trouble? Go to Jesus. Transport yourself in thought to the foot of the throne where He sits at the right hand of the Father, or throw yourself at the foot of the altar where He dwells, that He may be sacrificed to His Father and give Himself up to you. If you are a prince like Jairus, who was the Prince of the Synagogue, humble yourself, acknowledge the majesty, power, and goodness of Jesus; lay before Him your wants and your desires. He can do all He wishes; all He wishes is your good.

**Prayer:** Jesus, why do I not fly to Thee in the moment of trouble? Thy only thought in heaven, or upon our altars, is to succour us.

**Practice:** Often visit Jesus, present in the most Blessed Sacrament.

ಬಾಣ⊕ೞೞ

## 380 ~ Monday

**"Lord, my daughter is even now dead; but come, lay Thy hand upon her, and she shall live." ~ St. Matthew (9:18)**

**Thought:** Even is your soul is dead to grace by sin, go to Jesus, say to Him, "Lord, my soul has lost its spiritual life, lay but Thy hand upon me, and my soul shall live again."

**Prayer:** Jesus, remember that Thou didst come down from heaven, that Thou still dwellest upon our altars to save mankind. Take pity, then upon my misery.

**Practice**: Have recourse to Jesus when you have committed any fault.

ഇ൫൩⊕ഌൟ

## 381 ~ Tuesday

**"And Jesus, rising up, followed him, with His disciples."** ~ St. Matthew (9:19)

**Thought:** Be prompt and ready to oblige. Actions are better than words. Jesus rises without a word and follows the Prince of the Synagogue. As in the speech of Our Lord, so in His conduct, we may notice a precision and a decision both calm and rapid, strong and mild, which is a mark of God.

**Prayer:** Jesus, grant that I may follow the inspiration of zeal and charity with docility and promptitude.

**Practice**: Do not hesitate a moment when there is question of honouring God, or serving our neighbour.

ഇ൫൩⊕ഌൟ

## 382 ~ Wednesday

**"If I shall touch only His garment, I shall be healed."** ~ St. Matthew (9:21)

**Thought:** In Holy Communion we not only touch His garment, that is the Eucharistic veil beneath which He is concealed, we not only touch God Himself, but we become united to, incorporated with, Him, or rather He unites Himself to and  is incorporated with us.  Thus do we become, in a still more real manner, living members of that Body called the Church whose Head and Chief is Jesus Christ.

**Prayer:** Jesus, by Thy contact with me in Holy Communion, cure me of my weaknesses, my languor, and my miseries.

**Practice:** Have boundless confidence in the almighty power of God present to us in Holy Communion.

ಜಞ❀ಞಚ

### 383 ~ Thursday

**"Be of good heart, daughter, thy faith hath made thee whole." ~ St. Matthew (9:22)**

**Thought:** Jesus can refuse nothing to faith.  His word and honour are pledged to it.  His word, inasmuch as He has proclaimed a hundred times that all things are possible to him who believes.  His honour, for how could Jesus abandon any one who confides in Him?  Otherwise He would compromise His truth, His goodness, and His power.  Jesus can save me.  He desires my salvation, He has promised me it; I know it and believe it.

**Prayer:** Jesus, I believe, but strengthen my faith; I hope, but increase my confidence.

**Practice:** Act according to the spirit of faith, relying rather on the infallible word and almighty goodness of Jesus, than on your own strength and efforts.

ജ്ഞ❀ങ്ങ

## 384 ~ Friday

**"Give place, for the girl is not dead, but sleepeth."** ~ St. Matthew (9:24)

**Thought:** All hope apparently is lost. Yes, humanly speaking, the perfection to which you aspire is unattainable, the work you have undertaken cannot be done, nevertheless, continue to hope. This death is only apparent: had it been real, it will be so short that it will be no more than a slumber.

**Prayer:** Jesus, we are lost without Thee; but with Thee all is gained. My only hope is in Thee.

**Practice:** When the world mocks you and laughs to scorn your confidence in God, persevere and trust in Him.

ജ്ഞ❀ങ്ങ

## 385 ~ Saturday

**"And when the multitude was put forth, He went in and took her by the hand, and the maid arose."** ~ St. Matthew (9:25)

**Thought:** Are you desirous that Jesus should

enter into your soul? Drive out the multitude, expel those many thoughts, that crowd of recollections, that multitude of desires, those innumerable passions. The hand is the instrument of actions; without Jesus your works are dead; your hand once touched by the hand of Jesus regains life; you actions joined to those of Jesus will become actions of life.

**Prayer:** Jesus, drive from out my mind and heart all that vexes and troubles me, all that hinders me from hearing Thy voice or receiving Thy influence. Take me by the hand and raise me up, otherwise I must remain motionless, senseless, as the dead.

**Practice:** Be guided by Jesus.

ಬಲಾ ✤ ಚ೭ಚ3ಬಲಾ ✤ ಚ೭ಚ3ಬಲಾ ✤ ಚ೭ಚ3

## 386 ~ Twenty-Fourth Sunday After Pentecost

### "He that readeth, let him understand." ~ St. Matthew (24:15)

**Thought**: Just as the material world is a book, so is the social world. One can read the future by the present. The revolutions of our time are only types of that final revolution which will bring with it utter ruin to the wicked, eternal triumph to the just.

**Prayer:** Jesus, enlighten me, that I may now judge persons and thing as Thou wilt judge them at the Last Day.

**Practice:** Recognise the hand of God in passing events.

ಉಜ಼ು಼⊛ ಲ಼ಲಚ

## 387 ~ Monday

### "For there shall be then great tribulation."
### ~ St. Matthew (24:21)

**Thought:** There is no victory without a battle. Great tribulation announces and prepares the way for great manifestations of the wisdom, goodness, and justice of the Almighty King. The elements may unite, nations may be overthrown, you have only to place your trust in God, and you will be tranquil in the tranquillity of God Himself.

**Prayer:** Jesus, what need I fear from man? What have I to fear from the elements? Thou who art Master of the one and the other wilt know how to protect those who belong to Thee.

**Practice:** Be calm in the midst of tribulation.

ಉಜ಼ು಼⊛ ಲ಼ಲಚ

## 388 ~ Tuesday

### "For there shall rise false Christs and false prophets." ~ St. Matthew (24:24)

331

**Thought:** The most fearful of all tribulations will be that of false doctrine. Error, especially in religious matters, is the most deadly of all scourges. Famine, pestilence and war take life from the body. Passion, human respect and vice degrade and enslave the heart; yet so long as the principles of faith remain there is hope. When once the mind is corrupted, the intellectual, moral, and religious life is gone forever.

**Prayer**: Jesus, teach me to combat falsehood, to unmask false prophets, and to confound the impious.

**Practice:** Zeal for the propagation of good books.

ುಜಿ ✺ ಝಚ

### 389 ~ Wednesday

**"Wheresoever the body shall be there shall the eagles also be gathered together."**
**~ St. Matthew (24:28)**

**Thought:** The Body of Jesus is upon the cross, there to be immolated; it is also upon the altar, there to be Victim and nourishment for us; again, It is in Heaven reposing there in glory; *in fine*, we shall see the Body of Jesus descending on a brilliant cloud at the Day of Judgement. Wherever Jesus is He draws towards Him the eagles, i.e., those pure, brave souls, those minds whose sight is pure and fine, those wills whose flight is strong and rapid.

**Prayer:** Jesus, teach me to fly incessantly towards Thee in thought, memory, and desire.

**Practice:** Often pay a visit to the most Blessed Sacrament.

ಏಜಾ❀ಚಾಚಿ

## 390 ~ Thursday

**"And then shall appear the sign of the Son of Man in Heaven." ~ St. Matthew (24:30)**

**Thought:** The Cross is the sign, the standard of Jesus Christ. Who are they that shall be called to range themselves under this noble banner? Those marked with the sign of the cross, those for whom this sacred sign has not been merely a simple ceremony; those who have carried the cross, who have suffered, who have been humbled, who have been crucified.

**Prayer:** Jesus, inspire me with love for the cross and courage to carry it  Thou savest souls by the cross alone; I cannot be saved, nor can  save others, without it.

**Practice:** Make the sign of the cross with faith and confidence.

ಏಜಾ❀ಚಾಚಿ

## 391 ~ Friday

**"And they (His angels) shall gather together His elect from the four winds."**
**~ St. Matthew (24:31)**

**Thought:** See the elect now risen and the glorious standing round Jesus. Not one particle of their ashes that has not been found by the angels! Thus nothing pertaining to the Body of Jesus, which is the Church, can be lost. Every single good thought, word, action, and desire, will be remembered at the Day of Judgement.

**Prayer:** Jesus, grant that I may not lose one instant of this temporal, fleeting life, so that in the next life these fleeting instants may be changed into so many degrees of eternal glory.

**Practice:** Let us not lose an instant – time is short.

ಜಿಜಿ ✿ ಲ ಲ

"Heaven and earth shall pass, but My words shall not pass." ~ St. Matthew (24:35)

**Thought:** What folly it is to work for fortune or glory, which with heaven and earth must pass away. Nothing is solid save what is built upon the Word of God. Every thought, word, and action which does not tend to the glory or service of Jesus Christ is vain and useless.

**Prayer:** Jesus, I will imitate Thy word and example.

**Practice:** Despise the world and all passing things.

FINIS